Trading in Gold

How to Buy, Sell, and Profit in the Gold Market

by Paul Sarnoff

SIMON AND SCHUSTER • NEW YORK

Published by Simon and Schuster
A division of Gulf & Western Corporation
Simon & Schuster Building
Rockefeller Center
1230 Avenue of the Americas
New York, New York 10020
Original edition published in 1980 in Great Britain
by Woodhead-Faulkner Limited
SIMON and SCHUSTER and colophon
are trademarks of Simon & Schuster
Manufactured in the United States of America
1 2 3 4 5 6 7 8 9 10
Library of Congress Cataloging in Publication Data
Sarnoff, Paul.
    Trading in gold.
    Includes index.
    1. Gold.   2. Gold buying.   I. Title.
HG293.S27   332.6'3   80-21725
ISBN 0-671-41329-5

Contents

Trading in Gold

1

Introduction

> They wonder much to hear that gold, which in itself is so useless a thing, should be everywhere so much esteemed, that even men for whom it was made, and by whom it has its value, should yet be thought of less value than it is . . .
>
> Sir Thomas More

The purpose of this book

Since Biblical times, stories, poems and books have been written about gold, depicting the drama and the excitement of gold exploration, mining, smuggling, thefts—and other legal and illegal activities associated with man's eternal quest for private enrichment through acquisition of the 'Midas metal'. Probably Timothy Green's book, *The World of Gold Today* (Walker & Co., New York, 1973), is one of the most edifying and entertaining works of this nature.

But *Trading in Gold* does not dwell in great detail on where gold comes from or where it goes. Nor is the history of gold in its various forms before the end of 1974 mentioned—except where necessary.

Instead, this book tries to provide sensible strategies, trading methods and systems that could help alert traders and speculators to glean profits in a very volatile price medium—and also suggest an approach to price protection for commercial firms and users who require hedging transactions applicable to inventory and usage.

In this regard the work has been pragmatically partitioned into chapters that are independent and restricted to specialized topics.

1

Chapter 2, for example, deals with gold forms and facts—basic information that may be useful to anyone interested in gold. Chapter 3 enlarges on the various kinds of gold trading media; and Chapter 4 describes gold trading markets. Thereafter aspects of trading in gold futures are explained—with suggestions for profits and protection for both bullishly and bearishly inclined traders.

For readers reluctant to invest in bullion, coins or jewelry, and who have reservations about the speculative risks of the futures markets, Chapter 9 provides an examination of profit opportunities in both gold shares and the so-called 'gold funds'. In subsequent chapters gold trading systems, and the outlook for the metal as we head toward the next century, are discussed. Whenever possible, actual case histories, illustrations and tables are used.

Finally, since the whole subject is full of technical terms and unfamiliar expressions, I have included a glossary which explains the special features and language of gold trading in more detail than is often possible in the text.

The recent history of gold trading in the United States

Before embarking on the specifics of how to make money (or lose it) by trading in one form of gold or other, it is fitting to use some '20/20 hindsight' and allude to events that have led to the greatest precious metals bull markets in history.

The trigger that set off the excitement in gold trading actually occurred on the last trading day in 1974, when Americans—after a gold ownership ban since 1933—were once again permitted to own gold bullion legitimately. In addition, Americans were permitted to trade in gold futures, which simultaneously made their debut both in New York and Chicago at that time.

For years prior to the end of 1974, gold futures in 400 ounce contracts had been trading on the Winnipeg Exchange, but Americans were not legally permitted to go long in futures on that exchange prior to the end of 1974. Since at that time Winnipeg had only a 400 ounce gold futures contract (it currently offers a 'centum' 100 ounce contract) and the American gold exchanges offered trading opportunities in 100 ounces or less (New York Mercantile began with a one kilogram contract, Chicago Board of Trade with three kilograms, etc.) the commodity exchanges in

America had a definite advantage over the Canadian exchange—and a very brisk business began right from the outset.

The debut of gold futures trading in America was accompanied by the massive effort to retail gold bullion bars in various sizes to its citizens. Mocatta Metals made a pact with a large stock brokerage firm (Drexel Burnham) to form a corporation called the Mocatta Metals Corporation whose mission was to 'sell gold to Americans'. Merrill Lynch made a partnership with Samuel Montagu, a member of the London gold market (Merrill Montagu), to sell physical gold to Americans. Bache went into the gold retailing business. And so it went on—with confidence and high hopes that Americans would become as emotionally attached to gold, after such a long drought, as Europeans traditionally have been.

But something went wrong. From the end of 1974 to 1976 the dollar was relatively stable abroad and the inflation rate in America appeared under control—at least for the necessities of life. While the gold bullion vendors attempted to convince Americans that gold should become a part of every investor's portfolio, the efforts turned out to be mainly in vain as the price of gold dropped from a summit of close to $200 an ounce to $103 during the years that followed. And then the picture underwent a rather radical change.

In 1976—and during the years 1977 and 1978—the South African agency responsible for distribution of Krugerrands began a massive advertising campaign to attract Americans to its gold coins. The epitome of the theme involved in the advertising emerged in the third quarter of 1978 when advertisements appeared in America showing a married, middle-aged couple, in a rowing boat, with a giant ocean wave about to descend on them. The wave, of course, was labeled 'Inflation' and the wife was asking the husband: 'Henry, weren't you going to put some of our savings into gold?'

Evidently, since 1976, when inflation began to destroy the purchasing power of the US dollar at home—and especially during 1978, when attacks in the foreign currency markets made the dollar decline abroad—gold has been sought as a hedge against rising prices. Today, perhaps the affinity for gold in some form or other may be becoming too strong, causing people to invest in the wrong forms of gold. Americans, both male and

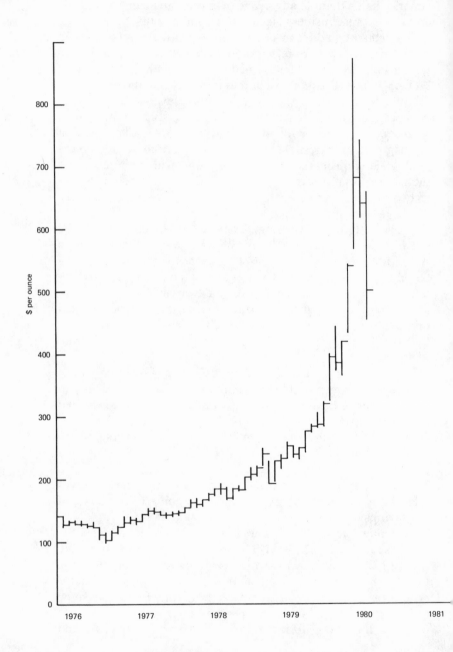

Fig. 1.1 Monthly fluctuations in the price of gold on the New York Comex, January 1976–March 1980 (data copyright of Conti-Commodity Technical Research Department)

female, are wearing more gold jewelry than any other people, the United States is now the largest market in the world for gold bullion coins and gold futures trading and the pioneering efforts of the December, 1974, gold vendors have finally caught on.

Fig. 1.1 illustrates monthly gold price fluctuations from January, 1976, through March, 1980. Notice that from the fall of 1976 through the first few months of 1980, the gold price trend was decidedly up. During 1979, minor downtrends provided bears with occasional opportunities for in-and-out profits. Basically, however, trading gold from the long side and holding it proved the best attack for profit-minded speculators and investors—that is until the collapse in precious metals prices during February and March, 1980.

While the gold price rise during 1979 may be attributed to inflation, fueled by the rising cost of oil, the sharp rise in the last few months of 1979 and the initial month of 1980 can be credited to the sudden entrance of American and foreign investors who became fearful the dollar wouldn't be worth even the paper it is printed on.

And the collapse, of course, came from a) the sudden rise in the American prime rate toward the 20% level; and b) a tightening of credit by the Federal Reserve. The cost of carrying physical gold on margin became oppressive and liquidation occurred. In addition, the mass liquidation of silver futures and physicals belonging to investors with very large holdings also managed to pull down the gold price drastically during February and March. But in my opinion, these were highly abnormal markets where the involved commodity exchanges deliberately set out to stifle speculation in order to forestall price manipulation.

Obviously, the actions of the exchanges were greatly influenced by Governmental agencies; and it is interesting to recall Treasury action and policy with regard to the monthly gold auction, that eventually was halted—without any admission by the government of such stoppage—in November, 1979.

Fig. 1.2 shows the fluctuation in value of April, 1979, gold futures during the period January 1978–January 1979. Notice that the major trend reversed for a very brief period as the price of gold plummeted down to about $193 in London ($196 on the April futures chart) before resuming its upward price climb. The temporary drop in gold price, of course, was a direct result of President Carter's massive monetary intervention plans designed

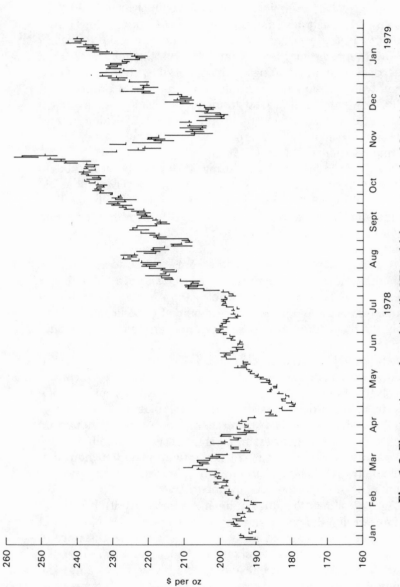

Fig. 1.2 Fluctuating value of April 1979 gold futures on the New York Comex, January 1978–January 1979 (data copyright of Conti-Commodity Technical Research Department)

to prop the dollar. But as the world realized such proppings could not be long-lasting, without correction of the inflation disease in America, the basic up-trend resumed.

Ironically, the United States has for some time attempted to divorce the importance of gold as a monetary metal from the international scene. To provide financial cosmetics to its balance-of-payments deficit, the United States had increasingly sold larger and larger amounts of gold at its monthly auctions, currently suspended. A US Treasury spokesman explained:

> These sales served three important US objectives:
> 1. They helped reduce the US trade deficit, which has been a major factor in the weakness of the dollar.
> 2. They responded directly to conditions in the gold markets, which have contributed to adverse psychological atmosphere in the foreign exchange market which has undermined international monetary stability.
> 3. They promoted the internationally agreed effort to reduce gradually the monetary role of gold.

Alas, the reasoning of the Government spokesman was rather bizarre. Because the United States considered gold sold at its monthly auctions as 'exports' it did help the outlook for the balance of payment deficit. Thus, about 14 million ounces of gold have disappeared from the Treasury. The gold reserves of the United States have been lessened and, if sales had continued at the 1979 rate, then in a bit more than fifteen years the Treasury would have had no gold and I shudder to think of what the dollar would be worth at that time.

Secondly, the reference to the foreign exchange market that has 'undermined monetary stability' is merely an example of the kind of attitude aired in the press. The key factor in dollar weakness is not the trade deficit, but rather the inflation rate inside the United States. In Switzerland, in early 1980, the rate was about 2% a year; in West Germany, about 4%; and in Japan about 5½%. In the United States, the admitted inflation rate in the spring of 1980 was 18%, but private experts deemed it to be closer to 25%. So in retrospect, selling Treasury gold does not 'stabilize' foreign exchange markets but instead provides buyers with bullion at a discount from where the gold price will be someday if inflation continues unchecked. This view is supported by the fact that on average since the gold auctions made their debut in May, 1978, and until they were suspended in November, 1979, the auction price had stood at about $2 below the second London fixing on the day of the auction in question.

Since the monthly gold auctions exerted so much influence on the market, traders and speculators will be keeping a watchful eye on what the United States government will be doing about resuming or not resuming its auctions. They will also be watching to see what stability ensues from the operations of the European Monetary System, which has a 20% gold reserve in its makeup.

Having touched upon a bit of price history, it is now fitting to turn to the various forms of gold and some pertinent facts about them.

2

Gold forms and facts

Of all the forms in which gold has been used to enhance humans over the ages, probably gold rings—especially wedding rings—have been the most publicized and popular. But, in fact, gold rings and other forms of jewelry labeled with the description 'gold' are rarely fashioned from pure gold. Usually, the gold has been alloyed with other metals, including copper and silver.

Obviously, the value of a piece of jewelry is not restricted to the amount of noble metal contained, but may also include a *premium* (price above the actual gold value) because of design, craftsmanship, antiquity and so on. For example, the treasures of King Tut would command an almost unimaginable premium above their actual gold content; and Cellini's salt cellar, fashioned out of solid gold, is probably one of the most priceless possessions on earth.

Now while not all of us are fortunate enough to have inherited priceless heirlooms consisting of some percentage of gold, the chances are that almost everybody has gold in some form or other around the house, including watches, spectacle frames, jewelry, and coins. All of the gold in such forms can be converted into cash—in whatever country in the world the owner happens to be, because gold in *any form* has always been considered a storehouse of value.

Interestingly enough, the forms of gold in times of demand normally should command a premium over the gold bullion itself due to the cost of manufacture and so on. Still, when attempting to sell gold in forms other than bullion or bullion coins, or futures, the owners encounter what the trader would call the 'spread'. That could be alluded to as the *premium* when a person intends to buy and the *discount* when trying to sell. Moreover, certain forms of gold are more liquid than others and so entertain a more ready market.

But before dwelling upon the liquidity or the non-liquidity of gold in its various forms, I shall first list the yardsticks of gold content and then list the attributes and the disadvantages of owning gold in any of the various forms, because this book, after all, is intended for gold traders and not for antique collectors.

The measurement of gold

Gold has an atomic weight of 197, is atomic number 79 in the table of elements, has a melting point of 1,064°C, and its specific gravity of 19.3 makes it rather burdensome to tote around in large quantities.

Gold jewelry is traditionally labelled in karats. A karat is a unit of fineness for gold equal to a 1/24th proportion of pure gold. Thus, if a piece of jewelry is labeled '18 karats' (18K) it is 75% (18/24th) gold. If it is labeled '10 karats' (10K) then the gold content in the alloy so labeled is 10/24ths pure, and so on. The following table illustrates popular gold jewelry alloys and their gold content:

Karat count	Purity	Jewelry origin
24 Karat	100%	Indian jewelry
22 Karat	91%	Indian jewelry
18 Karat	75%	European jewelry
14 Karat	58%	American jewelry
10 Karat	41%	American jewelry

In addition to the percentage of gold content inside the piece of jewelry to be sold or bought, the purchaser or seller is, of course, interested in the actual weight of the gold contained in the piece in question.

Gold, like silver, platinum and palladium, traditionally has been weighed according to the troy system of measurement. The following table illustrates the system:

1 troy pound	= 12 ounces, 240 pennyweight, 5760 grains
1 troy ounce	= 20 pennyweight, 480 grains
1 pennyweight	= 24 grains, 0.05 ounces
1 grain	= 0.042 pennyweight, 0.002285 ounces

For metric devotees, a troy pound is 0.373 kilograms; an ounce is

31.103 grams; and a pennyweight is 1.555 grams. All ounces quoted in this book are troy ounces.*

Gold jewelry

Keeping this system of weights in mind—and remembering that physical gold in early 1979 was around $250 per ounce—it is interesting to note what owners of gold jewelry could have received if they had taken their treasures out of the vault and had decided to sell them for the gold content. A spring 1979 advertisement by enterprising storekeepers in America seeking to help their fellowmen and fellowwomen turn inanimate objects into ready money offered the following prices:

10K gold	$3.35 per pennyweight
14K gold	$5.05 per pennyweight
18K gold	$6.15 per pennyweight
22K gold	$6.75 per pennyweight

Referring to our previous table, it becomes clear that 20 pennyweights (1 ounce) of 22K gold sold at the advertised price by an uninformed seller would net him or her the paltry pittance of $135. But the gold buyer would have stood to realize $227.50 at the price at that time of $250 an ounce for pure (24K) gold.

Now you may rightfully ask 'What about the artistry involved in the gold jewelry resold?' or 'What about the age and the sentiment behind the piece?' And the answer to both questions is simply that sources advertising that they will buy gold in any form generally are not connoisseurs, collectors or philanthropists. Rather, they are hard-headed business people who want to make a living from the need of the jewelry owners and their general ignorance of the values (and greed), and from the inexorable pressure of inflation.

So, if the reader does not have to part with gold jewelry that has been artistically fashioned, it might be wise to avoid generating cash through such methods. After all, jewelry gold is not allergic, it remains without tarnish over the centuries, and will always complement the beauty of the wearer.

Gold coins

The second largest area of acquisition for gold investment by

---

* A troy ounce is 1.097 ounces avoirdupois; a troy pound is 13.17 ounces avoirdupois; a pennyweight is .05486 ounce avoirdupois.

Americans since the end of 1974 has been the purchase of bullion coins. And it is likely that this form of anti-inflation hedging has been quite popular in Britain and on the Continent, as well as elsewhere in the world, even Abu Dhabi. Gold in coin form is available in two broadly categorized divisions, collector coins and bullion coins.

Collector coins are those that were specially struck by various countries, including the United States, and which are currently vended at ever-increasing premiums over their gold content because of limited supply and demand. While transactions on the buy and the sell side of such coins as the Czarist Russian Roubles are limited to coin shops and to other interested collectors, and auctions, there are some coins which originally were struck for circulation by various countries and which are now considered to lie somewhere between the bullion coin and the collector coin status because these coins will never be issued again by the various governments but are still in sufficient supply to make a fairly liquid market on both sides of the Atlantic. Such coins include the US $10 and $20 gold pieces, the British Sovereign, the French Napoleon and the Austrian Kroner.

A bullion coin, on the other hand, is simply a substitute for gold bullion and carries very little or no premium above the value of its gold content. Since the end of the gold ban for Americans, South Africa has busily been striking Krugerrands, the most popularly known and advertised bullion coin, usually shortened to 'Krugers'; Mexico has been issuing its 50 Peso gold coins; and Austria has been restriking its 100 Kroner coin, whilst Great Britain has been issuing its Sovereigns with the likeness of the current Queen on the face. As will be demonstrated in the next chapter, it is my contention that bullion coins are not only a manner of owning gold preferable to any other physical forms but are also—at least for the person of modest means—the only medium that should be traded if physical acquisition is paramount in the trader's mind.

In this regard I may encounter some objections from traders and hoarders who believe buying gold bullion is a better means of hedging against inflation than piling up gold coins in a systematic manner. But since we are going to analyze and compare the merits and disadvantages of each form from a trading standpoint in the next chapter I shall conclude this chapter with some comments on gold bullion itself.

Gold bullion

Bullion is gold in bar form; bars are *cast* for sizes of one kilogram upwards, and usually stamped for smaller sizes (one ounce, etc.). When the long-standing ban against American ownership of gold bullion ended at the end of 1974, several enterprising companies on both sides of the Atlantic almost simultaneously launched a program permitting Americans to buy and accumulate gold bullion.

As has already been mentioned, heading this drive to sell gold to Americans were combinations of Mocatta Metals and Drexel Burnham, Merrill Lynch and Samuel Montagu, and others. Gold bullion of 995 fineness or 999 fineness (see below) was made available at various locations, for example Wilmington, Delaware, in the United States and Geneva and Zurich on the Continent. The sizes of such bullion ranged from the standard 400 ounce bars good for London gold market delivery to 1 ounce 'ingots'. (The most popular gold sizes are castings—from 1 kilo to 400 ounce bars—while the smaller sizes—1 ounce, 5 ounces, etc.—are generally stampings. In 1979 Bache emerged as a gold bullion supplier of its own bars of 10 ounce size.)

While at first the efforts of those who wanted to sell gold to Americans seemed to be succeeding, the business declined because of two major deterrents: the price of gold dropped in an increasingly downward trend for the two years following the end of the gold ban and various US states saddled prospective gold buyers who were residents with rather expensive *sales-and-use* taxes. Some buyers avoided paying the tax by buying the bullion and storing it out of the resident state; but if they eventually wanted possession of the bullion they would of course have had to pay the tax, etc.

Another important consideration for holders of bullion involved storage and insurance charges. While these at most are actually quite moderate they still are real expenses that the hedger against inflation has to undergo while waiting for a long-term gain to appear when the bullion is eventually sold.

The facts about gold bullion are rather simple. In the London gold market, the world's most liquid physicals market, bars that constitute good delivery are 400 ounces of no less than 995 gold (i.e. 99.5% purity, equivalent for most purposes to 24K). Thus accumulators of bullion in less than 400 ounce bars would have to bear an added premium, if they wanted to sell the physicals to the London market. But delivery on the New York Comex Exchange, the Chicago Mercantile or the Chicago Board of Trade involves 100 ounce bars of at least 995 quality and so accumulators of that size and purity could probably get better treatment if they sold their physicals as part of closing out their open short positions in the gold futures traded on the respective exchanges, by delivering instead of offsetting.

In addition to the problem of proper size and purity, the bullion holder who intends to deliver into any of the gold markets in America or abroad has to be able to authenticate both the weight and the purity of the gold being delivered. This is often problematic unless the bars bear the weight and the fineness markings, and the stamp of the refiner and/or bullion dealer involved. Irrespective of the quality of the authenticity (i.e. the confirmation of the gold content), if the bars are delivered by other than the widely known and respected bullion dealers or refiners, the sale and delivery is 'subject to examination'. This examination can be quite detailed and expensive in the case of large shipments. Random bars, for example, are sawn into pieces and assayed to make sure the fineness and the weight are appropriate. The gold delivery people have a distortion of the adage: 'Trust everybody, but cut the cards.' Their version is 'Trust nobody and always cut the bars'. There is a mountain of entertaining literature about swindles involving gold bullion and one of the most humorous movies I ever saw, starring Alec Guinness, entitled *The Lavender Hill Mob,* had the thieves who stole a myriad of bullion melt it down and cast it into tiny Eiffel Towers that appeared quite golden and were to be shipped out of England under the description 'souvenirs'.

It is a characteristic of gold that it seems to lend itself quite readily to chicanery and fraud. In this regard it is wise therefore to deal *always* only with or through members of the various gold markets around the world, or with bullion dealers and brokers who are members of major stock and commodity exchanges. Buying gold bullion from companies with fancy names and frugal bank accounts is forever fraught with danger; buying gold from strangers who call on the 'phone or in person is a patent insanity. The gold business is certainly one where you cannot entrust your money to strangers or unknown firms or companies. In this regard it is wise to remember Mr. Dooley's dictum: 'If anybody offers you a sure thing, yell for a policeman'.

Of course, there is a sure way of owning and receiving properly weighted and pure bullion, and that is to go long in a gold futures contract on any of the North American exchanges and instead of closing out the open long position by offsetting it with a sale, take delivery. We will go into gold futures in more detail in the next chapter, but at this time it is proper to mention that buying the future and taking delivery is one way of assuring yourself you will get proper gold for the monies involved.

Conversely, the owner of gold bullion of a grade and an amount fulfilling the delivery requirements of the various gold future exchanges in America, can go short in the futures; and instead of offsetting his open shorts with covering buy orders, can actually make delivery. By doing this the trader can possibly realize a better price than by selling on the bullion market and in any case is assured of prompt payment when his gold is delivered according to exchange requirements.

The next chapter examines more closely, from the trader's viewpoint, the various gold forms and the desirability of trading in each.

3

Gold trading media

As a supplement to its regular regimen of reporting, *Business Week*, in the issue of 5 February, 1979, discussed 'investing' in gold, demonstrating 'six ways to put your money into gold'. Of course, we could not expect a popular magazine to delve into *all* the ways to speculate in gold, and obviously the use of the word 'investing' probably drew conservative readers who may have turned away from the article had the magazine chosen 'speculating', the proper term. The author of the article chose six gold trading media: Krugerrands, bullion, futures, stocks, jewelry and certificates. The items that were omitted from the foregoing 'investment' listing were gold options, leverage contracts and limited-risk forward contracts.

These omissions seemed quite bizarre in the light of the fact that, at the time of writing, in the United States Mocatta Gold Dealer options (puts, contracts to sell, and calls, contracts to buy) are the only legally permissible limited-risk ways of approaching the problem of earning leveraged profits in the gold price area. And leverage contracts (i.e. those using a little money to make a lot more), whilst currently undergoing investigation by the US Commodity Futures Trading Commission (CFTC), have not yet been banned. The only other bona fide limited-risk options on gold which are currently marketed outside the United States are the Valeurs-White Weld options, which were vended for years in the USA but were included within the CFTC ban of 1978. Valeurs has applied for permission to vend its options again in the United States but at the time of writing still has not received CFTC approval.

Since in my opinion the type of leverage contracts and limited-

16

risk forward contracts on gold sold in the United States at this time are simply thinly disguised substitutes for the banned options—and are generally vended by companies of questionable capital and character—it is best to assess them with a single word: *avoid*. Thus, there is no need to go into great detail as to how to try to profit from gold price movements in these questionable contracts. But we will go into greater detail a bit later with respect to the Mocatta gold options.

In the meantime, we will examine the merits of risking funds in the various gold-trading media from the standpoint of the trader.

Webster's Dictionary defines the word trader as someone whose 'business is buying and selling or barter'. But we will enlarge on this definition to include the person who attempts to profit from price changes in gold. In other words, we will add the dictionary definition of speculator to that of trader. Keeping this in mind, I now go on to evaluate the trader's best chances for profits among the gold trading media, beginning with gold bullion itself.

Gold bullion

Purchase of gold bullion requires one or both of the following:

(a) large committed capital;
(b) impeccable ready credit.

A single gold bar for delivery to the London bullion market at the going price of about $500 per ounce would require an outlay of $200,000. And since the best liquidity comes from a quantity between 2000 and 4000 ounces per order, the sums involved could run from $1 million to $2 million. Such orders would probably be filled at the London fixing at the time of the order, or with a very tiny premium.

Purchase of bars in lesser quantity than 2000 ounces, for example a 400 ounce bar involving $200,000, would bear a larger premium than the order for 2000 ounces. If the buyer wants 100 ounces in bar form, the premium would be higher than the one for the 400 ounce order, and so on. When purchasing bullion from a member of the gold market, the trader must realize he is conducting business with a *dealer*. And a bullion dealer, while impeccably honest, has expenses and must earn a profit on transactions to stay in business. It is quite understandable that in the bullion business, the smaller the bar the larger the premium, in percentage terms, and the ultimate cost to the bullion buyer.

Since the going price of gold is set twice a day in the fixings at the London gold market, all transactions for bullion all over the world are based upon these reference prices. Thus, purchase of 2000 ounces in London good delivery 400 ounce bars may be traded at about the fixing price ('the fix'), while a single 400 ounce order, may be 50¢–$2 per ounce over the fix, and 100 ounce orders may call for a $3 per ounce premium over the fix, and so on.

The minimum size purchasable from bullion dealers is usually one kilogram (slightly less than 33 ounces). Since the end of 1974 bullion has been available for Americans, Europeans and Asians in forms from one ounce to 400 ounce standard bars. If a person wants to accumulate a pile of gold bullion from monies that accrue over a period of years then he will be compelled to buy small bars, ingots or stampings on a regularly scheduled basis, according to cash flow, and perforce find himself paying a higher price overall than the fixings at purchase times. But in many cases this is the only way a small investor can accumulate a stock of gold.

Since gold is transportable, and good in any country in the world, it has also become a form of tax avoidance and a means of leaping currency restriction barriers set up by some of the nations. Two major problems involving transportability of gold bullion (some less polite authors might term it 'smuggling') are that gold is a heavy metal and that it must be authenticated as to weight and purity when a sale is contemplated. And, of course, there are fines and perhaps prison sentences for people who attempt to carry gold sewn inside their vests or skirts from one country to another and are caught at it. Since authentication, when selling has been accomplished, often slows the passage of funds from the buyer to the seller, we do not rate the trading in gold bullion for the small speculator or investor highly at all. In fact, for the person who approaches trading in the gold market with less than $1 million in cash and reserves we would suggest seeking alternatives, such as bullion coins, futures or options.

Bullion coins

Although bullion coins (Krugerrands, Kroner, Napoleons, Sovereigns, Francs, etc.) generally bear a higher premium in large quantities than standard bullion bars, they may have a lower premium than bullion in sizes of less than one kilogram. When dealing with coin stores, the buyer has to keep in mind that *caveat emptor* wasn't only for Romans. It is sensible to shop around for the best price. In America bullion coins are sold not only in coin stores, but may also be purchased from banks, stockbrokerage and commodity firms, and even jewelers. My own experience has been that the best price for bullion coins involves orders of at least 100 coins at a time and that orders for less than ten coins place the buyers in the same position as a customer paying the highest retail price around while the merchandise is being sold simultaneously at discounts elsewhere.

Nevertheless, I consider accumulation of bullion coins less expensive and far more sensible for buyers than the accumulation of bullion in small sizes. The prime reasons involve resale. When selling bullion back to a dealer the seller is compelled to wait for the proceeds until the dealer has examined to his satisfaction the shipment as to both accuracy of purity and weight of the gold. But in the case of coins they are readily identifiable and the seller may not experience the associated costs of assay and examination involved in the sale of bullion.

From the standpoint of a trader, of course, whether the item be gold bullion or bullion coins, it never makes much sense to take delivery from the bullion or coin dealer involved if the intention is simply to seek short-term profits (in less than a year or so).

Thus, a trader can purchase say 200 Krugers, or 200 Kroners through Mocatta or J. Aron, have them kept in safekeeping at a depository of the bullion firm, and then resell simply by making a 'phone call. But when buying from any bullion dealer or coin shop and accepting delivery, the buyer who later seeks to resell must understand that *all sales are subject to examination*. Counterfeiting bullion coins is indeed possible—and has been done both successfully and unsuccessfully—but a gold coin specialist can usually detect forgeries or mutilated coinage without the normally destructive assay.

Because of the widespread advertising campaign of the past few years the most popularly vended bullion coin in America is the Krugerrand, and this bears the highest premium to the buyer. I prefer the Austrian 100 Kroner, which unlike the Kruger does not contain exactly one ounce of fine gold but slightly less (33.8753 grams of 900 gold), and does not bear as high a premium. Thus if the Kruger bears a 7% premium for the buyer, the Kroner may only bear a 4% premium, and the same is true when it comes to the discount upon resale. Furthermore, even though the bullion coin is an adequate substitute for gold bullion it still has some collector possibilities because it is a coin.

In this regard the Krugerrand stands last when it comes to

Table 3.1 Gold bullion coins

Name of coin	Appreciation rating	Liquidity rating
South African Krugerrand	7	1
Austrian 100 Kroner	4	2
Mexican 50 Peso	5	3
Mexican 20 Peso	6	4
British Sovereign	3	5
French Napoleon	2	7
US Double Eagle ($20)	1	2

Notes: Rating 1 = best, 7 = worst. Appreciation rating in terms of possible future added value due to coin form over and above gold content. Liquidity rating in terms of readiness of buyers on resale.

bullion coins because the supply, at the time of writing, obviously will burgeon *ad infinitum* over the coming years, while the Austrian and the Mexican coins may not be continually restruck by their respective governments. The reason for this of course is that South Africa, which mints the Krugers as part of the nation's gold exporting program, is the world's largest source of gold ore, while Austria and Mexico have to import gold in order to fabricate the coins for exports.

At the time of writing, other nations around the globe, including Israel, Canada, Panama and the USSR, all want to get into the bullion coin export game—and the chances are that they will, because the demand doesn't look as if it will ever be sated. Like gold bullion, bullion coins can be used to transfer wealth without paying estate taxes, to jump international currency barriers and to constitute a convenient way of transporting wealth from place to place. It has been said that a million dollars' worth of Krugers at today's prices would fit easily in a safe deposit box; $2 million could go into a rather sturdy attaché case.

Table 3.1 lists the popular bullion coins, in descending order of their popularity with investors, along with my ratings of their appreciation possibilities and liquidity.

Gold jewelry

During the past ten years, jewelry accounted for just about 56% of all the gold used in the United States; and on a worldwide basis the consumption pattern for fabricated gold indicates that jewelry is still its dominant use.

In the United States, 10K and 14K dominates the field, with some objects fashioned from 18K gold. Abroad, and especially on the Continent, 18K gold objects are the most popular. Rings, bracelets, cuff links, chains, watchcases and mountings for precious stones and cameos predominate the jewelry markets; and recently there has arisen a rage for gold stickpins.

But very few of these adornments can be or should be risked as an investment in making money from trading gold. Of course, the intrinsic value of the metal in gold chains of an 18K content will rise as the price of bullion soars, but because the market is rather like the antique furniture market the buyer will suffer too much of a loss in value when attempting to resell. (By this I mean that very often people buy antique furniture at a high price and when they eventually go to sell it find they are being offered prices for second-hand furniture.)

Thus, while it makes sense to put some money in golden objects for adornment, we cannot recommend that money be risked at all in jewelry unless the risk-taker intends to retail the objects to some part of the public. For the trader or speculator who seeks to make profits from gold price fluctuations, investing in gold jewelry at normal prices doesn't make sense. Of course, should you find instances where estate or other jewelry is offered at distress prices then perhaps it is shrewd to accept the purchase. But in general if, when disembarking at a continental port, you are approached by someone who wants to sell you a 'gold' watch it is better to feign deafness and ignore the offer.

Gold medals, medallions and commemorative coins

In the United States, during the past few years, enterprising 'mints' have retailed millions of dollars' worth of medals and medallions commemorating various events, subjects and people. While the majority of these offers have been for silver, gold medals and medallions have also been advertised by mail and in the newspapers.

The fabrication and advertising costs, of course, are passed along to the purchasers, since these 'mints' are not in business to give anyone bargains. Naturally, the rationale behind the retailing efforts is simply that continued inflation will cause the medals and medallions to increase in value, owing to their gold content and the limited number of each issue struck by the mint. There is, of course, some measure of merit to this line of thinking but very often the purchaser finds that if cash is needed he or she would be fortunate to receive 35–50% of the original cost—even if the sale is some years after purchase. But this may not be true of collector coins, which have a growing market of their own and are outside the scope of this book.

There is a rather tenuous line dividing collector coins which were struck in the nineteenth and perhaps early twentieth century and the so-called commemorative coins now being struck by countries all over the world. Be that as it may, I would arbitrarily classify the coins struck by the Republic of Panama, called $100 gold Balboas (allegedly legal tender), and coins struck by the Soviet Union commemorating the 1980 Olympics as non-collector coins. An excellent example is the $1000 Hong Kong gold coin issued to celebrate the Year of the Goat (many Chinese call it the Year of the Ram). The Year of the Goat turns out to be a fine year to be born in because the goat (or the ram) is considered a symbol of good luck. Struck by the Royal Mint, these coins weigh 15.98 grams apiece and are 22K gold. Uncirculated coins were being sold for $225 each, at a time when the price of 995 gold was $250 per ounce. Reference to our tables on p. 10 indicates that these coins actually contain under ½ troy ounce of 995 gold, or less than $125 worth at the going rate at the time. It almost goes without saying that if you had bought any of these coins for $225 each, and wanted to sell them later, you would have had to wait for gold to reach over $450 per ounce just to break even, unless you sold them to someone else willing to pay the rarity premium.

So unless purchase of certain commemorative coins, medals and medallions is contemplated for sentimental or other sound reasons, including the intrinsic beauty of the craftsmanship, they are all outside the scope of the trader seeking profits from gold price changes.

Gold certificates

Obviously, when purchasing 2000 ounces of gold bullion through firms like Mocatta, J. Aron and so on one may decide to store the bullion at depositories of the bullion dealer; and upon payment one receives a certified warehouse receipt which is transferable. These certificates, like stock certificates, have forms on the back permitting legal transfer of the bullion involved.

There are also certificates sold by reputable companies such as

Mocatta which are termed 'DOs' (Delivery Orders). These are available in amounts under the 400 ounce standard bar and are also available for Krugers and Kroners.

The prime reason for such certificates involves the sales and use tax levied on the purchaser of gold bullion or bullion coins by many states inside the USA. For example, the purchaser of a 100 ounce gold certificate at say $500 per ounce would pay $50,000—and would be buying about $50,000 worth of gold. But if the gold was delivered, and if the purchaser lived in New York City, an 8% tax would apply to the purchase, for an added $4000. This, in fact, represents a penalty of $40 per ounce, and is far greater than any profit the bullion dealer might make on the deal. Most bullion dealers are content to make only a few dollars per ounce on orders of 100 ounces or less, while on large orders, an arranged commission or fee can be negotiated prior to purchase.

Full details of Mocatta's DOs appear at the rear of this book in Appendix B—and assuredly such orders may be effected with other reputable firms. The problem exists that to avoid state taxation there is the temptation to deal with firms that may be 'bucketing' (selling gold that does not exist). But dealing with people like the Swiss Bank, Valeurs-White Weld, Crédit-Suisse, and other reputable bullion firms that are allied with members of existing gold markets will preclude problems for the purchasers.

Trading in gold certificates therefore is a sensible way to approach the gold market providing you realize that you probably will be compelled to resell the gold stored at the bullion firm at the price offered by the firm to you when a sale is contemplated. And you should never buy certificates or send money to any firm for purchases of what is allegedly gold held in storage for your account unless you have thoroughly investigated that firm and found it to be reliable.

Gold shares and funds

Ever since Americans were legally able again to own gold bullion there has arisen great interest on the part of the investing and speculating public around the world in shares of gold mining and gold exploration companies, as well as mutual funds that specialize in so-called 'gold investments'.

Of course, on the stock exchanges around the world there are many issues of investment grade and of a speculative nature that are producers of gold ore or are involved in refining and distributing the actual metal, or are in the process of exploration and development of gold mines. In addition, and dating back into the nineteenth century in some cases, there is a whole host of companies, stretching from Canada to the Philippines, whose shares are virtually in the pennies. These marginal companies have made fortunes for a myriad of promoters past and present as the cookie jars and bank accounts of greedy but trusting souls have been emptied in vain hopes of striking Eldorado.

The gamut of gold shares ranges from those that have paid dividends for ages to ones that are on the brink of bankruptcy. And the dividend-paying ones in particular serve as a fine medium for investors seeking both long-term appreciation through the advancement of the gold price on world markets, and a satisfactory current yield or return on investment for taking the risk. Quite often the complaint is heard when considering investing in gold that the money will be tied up for years and will return nothing on the investment in the form of dividends or interest. So perhaps it makes sense for a trader to take a portion of the funds available for gold trading and invest in dividend-paying securities which are involved with gold in some significant manner. Then if gold declines temporarily in price while the trader is waiting for profits at least there will be some return on the money involved.

With this in mind I have devoted an entire chapter (Chapter 9) to gold shares and gold funds and will be far more explicit there than I am here. Suffice to say for the moment that gold shares do go up and down with the gold price but they are normally not nearly as volatile as the changing prices in the gold bullion or gold futures markets.

Gold futures

By definition a futures contract is one made between a buyer and seller in which the buyer puts down a small deposit (original margin) with his broker for the eventual purchase in full of the involved commodity. The seller of the contract deposits similar margin with his broker (popularly called a 'futures commission merchant' in the United States) as protection for the contract involving actual and eventual delivery of the commodity during the month specified. Of course, the buyer can offset his obligation by selling his contract prior to the delivery month and the seller can offset his delivery obligation by buying in a similar contract before the delivery month. The exchange where these futures are traded 'clears' the buy and sell sides of the transactions and demands 'interim maintenance margin' from either party if the price becomes adverse before the delivery month. This means that during declines the exchange will demand additional margin from the clearing broker and during price rises will pay equity to the broker. In retrospect, some 97% of all futures contracts ever made have been offset (liquidated by both buyers and sellers) before delivery and payment for the physical commodity was effected. Thus the futures market provides the greatest leverage for the gold trader and the least cost of carrying large amounts of gold over a specific period of time.

For example, the purchaser of 400 ounces of bullion at $500 per ounce would have to provide $200,000 and pay storage and insurance while owning the bullion if the bullion was left with the dealer. But assuming the buyer intended to own the bullion for one year and then liquidate for a profit or loss, depending on the price, he or she would have lost an additional sum of money on the funds locked up in the bullion. Since the United States Government in August, 1980, had to pay up to about 11% interest for borrowed funds, we can presume that the money use factor for one year for the bullion buyer then would have approximated $22,000! In other words, the price of his gold would need to go to at least $555 plus storage and insurance just to break even.

If instead of buying the bullion the risk-taker had positioned four contracts on the Comex in New York, a year out, his margin would have been $6000 per contract, or $24,000 in total. And had the trader deposited the balance of $176,000 in safe debt instruments (bonds, US Treasury Bills, etc.) he could have earned at least $19,360 interest on the money kept in reserve.

But what if the price of gold had declined during the year and more margin were demanded from the trader? As mentioned above, the exchange would demand margin from the clearing broker during declines and pay equity to the clearing broker during rises. So a buyer who was long in the gold futures could liquidate some of his reserve investments temporarily to supply maintenance margin when called and then return the money by drawing it out of his account with the clearing broker when the price rebounded. Whichever way you look at it, the buyer of four gold futures contracts who has the actual money to pay for the underlying gold bullion is better off than the risk-taker who plunks down $200,000 for the same amount of gold and leaves it lying at a dealer's warehouse for a year, paying for storage and insurance, and losing the use of the funds.

Recently one large firm, London Metal Exchange member Rayner-Harwill, inaugurated a substitute for gold futures in London, whereby the purchaser deposits 10% of the value of the gold purchased and the firm supplies the rest of the capital through financing. Thus the buyer is compelled to pay interest at going rates; and if the bullion is held for a year without significant appreciation the purchaser will be out of pocket on the interest and the other fees. Incidentally, since interest and storage are tax deductible in the United States, such leveraged* plans may have some appeal there. But trading in futures presents:

(a) the greatest leverage since the leverage is without cost;
(b) the least cost since only a small round-turn commission is usually involved (between $50 and $75 a contract);
(c) no extra risk, whether the trader actually owns 400 ounces of bullion paid for, or whether he holds four futures contracts with the pittance of a deposit and maintains a cash reserve on the balance that is earning money via investment for the period of time the futures are held.

While I may be rightly held as biased in favor of futures over any other form of gold trading there is still another form of trading in gold that I feel is equal or even superior to futures because it reflects *limited risk*. While the holder of bullion or futures can normally liquidate via a phone call at fairly reasonable prices, there is no way in the world to limit risk precisely without *options*.

Since there exist bona fide gold options that can be used for profit and protection no matter which side of the gold market the trader decides to be on (long or short) I shall conclude the chapter with a short discussion on that subject.

Gold options

A gold option is a contract made between buyer and seller in which the buyer pays a premium in money for the right to call away from the seller (grantor) a specific amount of gold at a specific contract price (strike price) at any time up to and including a set date (expiration date) in the case of a call; and in the case

---

* 'Leverage,' used here and elsewhere, is what British readers know as 'gearing.'

of a put the buyer pays premium for the right to deliver to the grantor a specified lot of gold bullion at an agreed strike price at any time up to and including the expiration date.

Obviously, such contracts depend on the ability of the grantor to fulfil the obligation assumed when he receives the buyer's premiums. So in effect every gold option is only as good as the company that endorses (guarantees) the contract. At this writing there are in my opinion only two broadly vended gold contracts worth considering: Mocatta Metals and Metal Quality puts and calls and Valeurs-White Weld gold calls.

The Mocatta calls are sold in the United States and cover 200 ounces of gold per contract based on strikes that vary in intervals of $20 each above and below the going price on the Chicago IMM; while the Valeurs calls, primarily sold on the Continent, involve five kilos (approximately 161 ounces) and are quoted in $10 intervals fairly close to the going price.

In other words, buyers can receive quotes on Mocatta calls at $500, $520, $540, etc.; or at $500, $480, $460, etc. when gold is trading at $500 for the involved contract month. The Valeurs calls in such a situation would be at $500, $510, $520; or at $500, $490 and $480, etc. Premiums for these calls vary with volatility of the gold price and the length of time covered by the option. In both cases, the grantors (Mocatta and Valeurs) stand ready to repurchase their options from holders if the holders decide to resell. While both grantors formerly offered very close spreads between the offering price and the buy-back price of their gold options, the volatility of the metal has caused the spread to widen. Thus Mocatta at one time had a spread of only $120 between its bid and offer and Valeurs had a spread of only $1 an ounce. Thus it was conceivable that a purchaser of a gold call who held it for only a day or so while the market didn't change very much could resell the option for a small loss. At this writing, Mocatta's spread is much larger than Valeurs and prospective purchasers should consider this before taking risks.

Thus it is conceivable that if one purchased such a call and gold did nothing much overnight, the call could be sold back to Mocatta for a small loss of $120, plus whatever the vendor's changes entailed. Valeurs maintains a spread of only $1.00 per ounce no matter what the premiums are.

Since gold options limit risk, and since they are also highly liquid, they do fit into a trader's approach if used sensibly together with futures and bullion. We will go into much more detail in Chapter 5 concerning usages and applications of options. For several years major exchanges in America have attempted to start up options trading in gold, silver, etc. on the same exchanges on which futures contracts in these metals are traded. But because of a plethora of problems, the Federal agency that supervises these exchanges has not seen fit to grant permission or formulate sensible rules regulating such trading. It is to be hoped that by the end of 1980 investors and speculators in gold will be able to indulge in both option buying and granting on these exchanges in a fair market, with open outcry and exchange clearances and guarantees, and have a choice of dealing there or with bullion dealers like Mocatta and Valeurs.

4

Gold trading markets

Physical markets

Gold is traded on a 24-hour basis practically all around the world. Traditionally, the world takes its pricing from the London gold market, which comprises five members: Mocatta & Goldsmid; Sharps, Pixley; N. M. Rothschild & Sons; Johnson Matthew; and Samuel Montagu & Co.

Until 1968, about 80% of the gold traded around the world passed through this market, including the gold shipped from South Africa. However, with the formation of the Zurich gold market in 1969, the bulk of physical transactions has shifted to that city. Now the gold from South Africa and most of the gold sold to the free world from the USSR is received there, and shipped to buyers or stored. The Zurich gold market is dominated by the Swiss Bank Corporation, Crédit-Suisse and the Union Bank of Switzerland. A good deal of their gold pool was purchased in 1968–69 at $35–$43 an ounce.

Of course, I do not wish to de-emphasize the importance of the London gold market, since the two daily fixings by the five members of that market are still the world standard of gold value. But, as most observers of gold markets admit, the greatest influence on the gold price each day is now exerted by what happens in the futures markets in gold, in America. In addition to London and Zurich as major gold bullion dealing centers, the other major physicals markets are Paris, Beirut, Tehran, Jeddah, Hong Kong, Singapore, Bombay, New York and Chicago.

Complementing these major markets, there are minor gold trading markets in virtually every large city around the globe, but

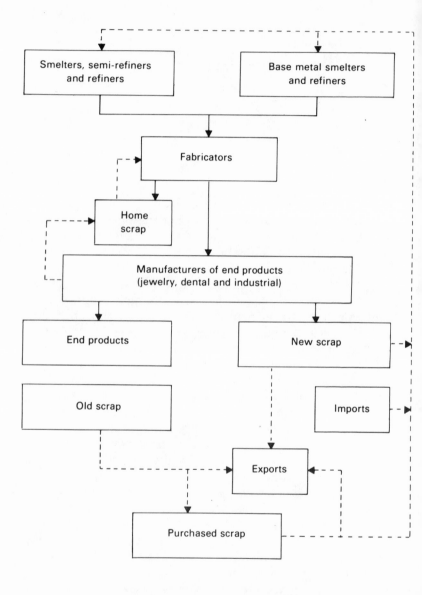

Fig. 4.1 Secondary gold flow (source: US Department of the Interior, Bureau of Mines)

the bulk of the business is understandably done in London, Zurich, Paris and New York.

Supplementing the flow of gold bullion from the mines to the users in cities around the globe is the trade in gold ore, concentrates and scrap. In many cases, gold also moves around the world as a component of unrefined copper. The general flow of gold in secondary industry is illustrated in Fig. 4.1.

Since we are not concerned here with trading gold in any other but the 995 purity form (in physical metal, futures or options contracts on the metal), it is sufficient to say there do exist profit opportunities for individuals and firms who may be attracted to secondary gold market operations. It takes both knowledge and money to succeed there. The *timing* of buying and selling scrap gold will ultimately be the deciding factor between success and failure after you obtain the needed ingredients of knowledge and money, if you explore this activity.

At one time people interested in buying gold bullion could have bid for it at the monthly auctions held by both the US Treasury and the International Monetary Fund (IMF). Currently the Treasury has halted its auctions without formally announcing that such auctions have ended. In fact, the Treasury let it be known that they have changed their policy and will auction when they feel the timing is right, and experts venture that when the Treasury ended its auctions it put several hundred dollars an ounce on the gold price. But the Treasury, when auctioning gold, accepted bids as low as 400 ounces, while the IMF required bids beginning at 1000 ounces. Forms had to be filed and a deposit of at least $10 an ounce had to accompany bids in order to be valid. For example, at the March 20, 1979, Treasury auction, one person filed a bid for 1 million ounces of fine gold at $300 an ounce; but since the bid was neither signed nor accompanied by a certified check for $10 million it was ignored and the metal went on the block at about $242 an ounce.

If you bid at a gold auction for government or IMF bullion and are awarded a lot of bullion covering the deposit, then the balance has to be paid within a week or ten days and delivery is effected at wherever the gold is stored. Transporting gold bullion in large quantities is a backbreaking and rather dangerous job that entails both trucking and insurance expenditures. When the gold bullion is finally in the hands of the owner, it must be stored in a safe place and again storage and insurance charges may substantially increase the cost of keeping the bullion for years.

This brings us to a rather startling conclusion: if you want to make money from gold, perhaps it is better never to take delivery of it, see it, store it or keep it. But the evidence is quite preponderant that gold can be a *great moneymaker to its owners in the various markets because of price changes.*

In this regard, the owner of gold bullion may never see his actual metal but is content to simply hold bona fide warehouse receipts. For example, a trader can purchase five-kilo lots of fine gold from Valeurs-White Weld in Geneva, store the metal there without charge and grant (sell) gold calls continually on his pile. The way current premiums have been running, the owner of the metal can approximate 20–30% per year on the gold kept in storage there.

In the case of an owner of gold futures contracts on the Comex or the Chicago IMM, or the New York Mercantile Exchange, which trades one kilo and also 400 ounce contracts, he or she can liquidate the contracts at higher levels for profits and then re-enter at lower levels, and so on. In most cases—especially in futures, where 97–98% of the contracts are never settled by delivery and payment but rather by liquidation via offset—the owners will never see, feel, or fondle the gold that made them the money.

This leads us on to the area of most interest to traders who are basically speculators and hunger to make money on money (their own and other people's).

Futures exchanges

The gold futures markets offer the highest degree of leverage and make the most sense, even if eventual ownership of gold bullion is contemplated. The major gold futures trading exchanges are located in New York and Chicago. In addition, exchanges operate in Winnipeg, Canada, Sydney, Australia, and Singapore. The Hong Kong gold market is a delivery market, similar to London, although at the time of writing there is developing an effort to promote gold trading in futures on that exchange. The Hong Kong market has always been the province of the Chinese Silver and Gold Society, and observers seriously doubt if gold futures will be initiated, or even if initiated, successful.

There can be little argument about the success of gold futures

Table 4.1 Gold futures markets

Exchange	Contract size	Minimum fluctua-tion	Daily limit	Value of $1 move	Trading hours (EST)
Chicago Board of Trade	100 oz	10¢/oz	$25	$1=$100	9.25–1.35
Chicago IMM	100 oz	10¢/oz	$25	$1=$100	9.25–1.30
New York Comex	100 oz	10¢/oz	$25	$1=$100	9.25–1.30
New York Mercantile	1 kg	20¢/oz	$25	$1=$32.15	9.25–1.30
	400 oz	5¢/oz	$25	$1=$400	
Winnipeg	400 oz	5¢/oz	$10	$1=$400	9.15–1.30
	100 oz	5¢/oz	$10	$1=$100	

Note: Gold is traded on the Sydney Futures Exchange, but such trading is restricted to Australian citizens. Gold is also traded in Singapore and Hong Kong but most futures are traded today in New York or Chicago.

contracts in America to date. Since their initiation in New York and Chicago at the end of 1974, the volume and interest in American gold futures contracts has grown amazingly, so that trading of 40,000 gold contracts on the Chicago IMM or the New York Comex in a single session is no longer a rarity. Table 4.1 is a listing of American gold futures markets, including pertinent trading information.

But before entering upon an explanation of what a gold futures contract is and how it can be used to advantage by speculators, traders and hedgers, as well as investors, it may help to introduce a flow diagram (Fig. 4.2) illustrating elements of a typical futures transaction.

The New York Commodity Exchange (Comex) is the largest metals futures exchange in the world and its genuine function is to act as a trading arena for buyers and sellers of futures contracts in the metals traded on that exchange. It trades gold, silver and copper futures. At the time of writing it has applied for permission to trade financial instrument futures. The Comex does not buy or sell any futures contracts, it merely provides the facilities for trading those contracts within established rules and regulations designed to provide fair and equitable treatment for the buyers and sellers of the contracts.

The buy and sell transactions occur from the meeting of bids and offers for specific gold futures contracts by open outcry at a

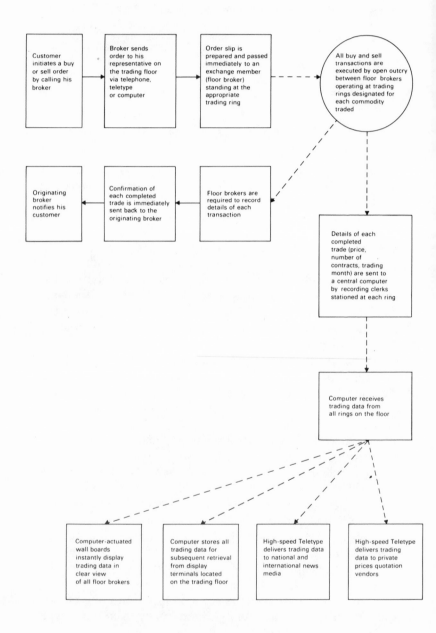

Fig. 4.2 Elements of a typical futures transaction (reproduced by permission of New York Comex)

trading ring set up on the exchange floor. Essential trading data, such as the opening, high, low and settlement prices, as well as the last four price changes, cumulative volume and trading limits are posted on electronic display boards overlooking the trading ring. All buy and sell gold orders on the Comex must be executed by a floor broker operating in the gold ring *during trading hours only;* and the exchange ticker system reports such trades and provides a continuous flow of price and volume information during the trading day.

The Comex gold contract calls for 100 ounces of gold assaying not less than 995 fineness, cast either in one bar or in three one-kilogram bars and bearing both a serial number and an identifying stamp of a refiner approved by the exchange. A list of approved refiners and assayers appears at the end of this book as Appendix A.

It is quite understandable that after a 'drought' of more than forty years, Americans would become emotionally attracted to gold bullion—especially since historically gold has been a source of refuge from paper during rabidly inflationary times. But few people realize that the début of the futures exchanges in America enabled massive amounts of gold already in storage somewhere in the world to be vended and delivered. So that actual owners of gold bullion during the past four years have had excellent forward markets in which to plan purchases and/or sales of the bullion.

So active a role did the exchanges play that by midsummer 1977 the United States became the world's largest center of gold marketing, with the focus on the New York and the Chicago exchanges.

In Chicago, the International Monetary Market (IMM) of the Chicago Mercantile Exchange led the way in activity for several valid reasons:

(a) its contract was similar to the Comex in that the contracts traded involved 100 ounces of the bullion;
(b) the Chicago Board of Trade (CBOT) gold contract involved three kilograms and people were not familiar with the metric system;
(c) the CBOT was the world's largest grain futures exchange and its members were primarily preoccupied with wheat, soya-beans, etc., rather than with metals.

But the IMM, which had already been active in making markets in foreign currency futures, had both the market-makers and the interest to lead the activity in gold futures trading in that city. Understandably enough, in the spring of 1979, the CBOT changed its gold contract to 100 ounces and perhaps its future as a trading arena for gold futures will burgeon. But to better explain the significance of gold futures trading one needs first to define and enlarge on the process.

A gold futures contract is a legally binding instrument to buy or to sell, say, 100 ounces of 995 bullion during a specific month at an agreed price made at the time of the transaction on the exchange floor. Both buyer and seller are required to deposit 'initial' or 'original margin' with their brokers and to maintain what is termed 'maintenance margin' thereafter until the contract is either fulfilled by actual delivery of the bullion involved or is liquidated by offsetting. If a trader buys a gold contract, he is 'long' and can either opt for delivery and receipt of the bullion at the contract price, or sell his contract on the exchange, thus offsetting his risk and liability. And if a trader sells (is 'short' in) a gold contract he has the option of either making physical delivery to the buyer during the spot month or offsetting his risk and contractual liability by purchasing a similar futures contract.

It naturally follows that speculators and traders who believe the price of gold is cheap will go long and hope to sell out at higher price levels if their theory is correct; and traders and speculators who believe gold will drop in price can go short and hope to buy-in their short position at a lower price, profiting thereby from the differential between where they sold and where they covered. Moreover, the trader long in gold must deposit an original margin at time of purchase and if the price *goes down* while the position is outstanding the owner has to pay additional, maintenance, margin. Conversely, the short trader or 'bear' has to deposit original margin and if the price of gold *rises* while the trader is short, his brokerage firm will demand maintenance margin.

We will enlarge on the details of these margins in the next chapter. It is sufficient to say here that the owner of a long gold future has the same downside risk as someone who has purchased and paid for 100 ounces of the bullion. The difference simply is that when buying the *future* he only has to deposit about $6000 for every 100 bullion ounces in which he is long, while a deposit of $50,000 approximately would be needed if gold *bullion* were bought at a price of $500 an ounce. And obviously, a rise of only $60 per ounce would be needed for the long to double his deposit money in the case of the future, while gold would have to go to $1000 an ounce to have a similar effect on the owner of the physical bullion.

The components of the futures market

The make-up of the gold futures market, unlike the physicals market contains more speculators than investors, since a speculator is primarily concerned with profits from price changes and futures provides him or her with the most chance for profits on the funds risked. Still, the basic market for gold futures trading, like Caesar's Gaul, can be divided into three distinct parts: the hedgers, the speculators and the bullion people (called brokers, but who also act for much of the time as dealers).

A hedger is a person or company that uses gold as part of a manufacturing or production plan. For example, in March a jeweler, who offers a large quantity of one ounce gold ingots as pendants for chains, would base his price on what gold would cost around next Christmas in the futures markets, and if he is successful in getting Christmas orders, would 'cover' his orders by purchasing (going long in) December gold in sufficient quantity to protect him from any price rise in the interim. If gold goes up, the jeweler will pay more when he orders the gold strips from which he stamps the so-called 'ingots' but he will have profited about the same amount he has to pay extra for the physical gold by selling his futures at the time of gold-strip purchase. This is called a *buying hedge*. The jeweler cannot make money, nor can he lose money if he is properly hedged and uses the futures market simply as 'price insurance'.

On the other hand, the owner of a gold mine may desire to 'pre-sell' his gold at a price six months out and goes short on the exchange for that month. If the market declines, the miner can deliver his gold at the pre-sold futures price or sell it at a lower price on the market and simultaneously cover his short future by buying to cover; and the money earned via this process will cushion the miner for the difference received on the physicals market. This is what is known as a *selling hedge*.

But by far the greatest activity on the futures exchanges involves speculators, whose concern is only with price changes. Those who think gold is cheap trade from the long side; those who think gold is too expensive go short and keep hitting the market on rallies, covering on dips. The 'gold-bull', of course, who trades from the long side, will buy on dips and sell on rallies. The presence of the speculator in ever-increasing numbers has provided gold futures exchanges with the kind of liquidity to be able to accommodate the vast quantities of gold sold at the monthly IMF auctions since June, 1976, and the Treasury auctions since May, 1978. In this regard, the use of futures markets to accommodate sales by bullion dealers has burgeoned.

It is immediately apparent that a bullion dealer will avidly bid at any gold auction if he has the ability to sell the gold he expects to be awarded at a higher-than-cost price. And the presence of bullion dealers at each and every auction and simultaneously in the pits of the various gold futures exchanges indicates strongly that the futures markets have been continuously used to hedge their auction purchases.

A final use of the exchanges is to facilitate purchase and/or sale of physicals. After all, the exchanges' strict requirements guarantee that warehouse receipts for metal only from approved refiners and assayers are available to buyers, and these receipts are the only kind acceptable from sellers. So if you want 100 ounces of metal without worrying about its authenticity simply buy a gold future on the IMM, Comex, or Winnipeg and accept delivery during the spot month.

To sum up, then, futures exchanges offer facilities for hedgers who are involved in physical production, processing, handling or marketing of gold; for speculators who are intensely interested in highly leveraged profits from price changes of the gold; and for buyers and sellers of physical gold who want ready markets and readily authenticated purity and weight of the gold bars involved. If the futures market provided no protective functions for the hedger it would be an uneconomic market; and without the speculator to assume the hedgers' risks there would be no futures market.

Now that we have touched upon some aspects of these important markets, in the next chapter I turn to the various strategies involved in making money with gold bullion, gold futures and gold options.

5

Gold trading strategies

The price of gold since 1974

When it comes to gold trading, the secret is simply to make money on the price fluctuations of gold, if possible. In this regard it is fitting to review briefly what happened to the price of gold since it became legal for Americans openly to own bullion at the end of 1974.

On December 31, 1974, when gold futures commenced trading in Chicago and New York, the London fix was $197.50. That price turned out to be the high for 1974—and for a long time to come. When 1975 made its début, the price of gold went into a long decline that reached its nadir at $103.75 per ounce in August, 1976. From that bottom, gold rose in price to reach what was then an all-time high of $254 on February 8, 1979. During the next two months, gold backed off to the $233 level.

It becomes immediately obvious that purchasers of bullion at the end of 1974 had to wait for a number of years just to break even. It is also obvious that on the way down as well as on the way up astute traders had plenty of opportunity to attack the problem of profits in gold futures by trading from the long side (buying on weakness and selling on strength), or trading from the short side (selling on strength and buying on weakness).

Moreover, the presence of the futures markets enabled owners of gold bullion to resort to 'cash-and-carry' strategies and to go short at times for protective purposes.

The relevance and purpose of this review of past experience is to educate readers about strategies that have worked previously and can be successfully applied to the future. One thing about the

Table 5.1 Gold futures prices on New York Comex and Chicago IMM at April 12, 1979

Comex

High	Low	Month	High/Low range			Net change	Open interest
258.80	170.00	Apr	233.70	232.30	233.00	+0.40	1,865
243.80	233.70	May	233.70	233.70	234.20	+0.40	32
263.80	164.20	June	236.50	234.90	235.60	+0.30	26,766
268.50	106.00	Aug	240.20	239.00	239.60	+0.30	10,186
273.50	183.40	Oct	244.50	243.00	243.70	+0.30	13,521
278.00	187.60	Dec	248.30	247.00	247.80	+0.30	22,911
283.00	190.50	Feb	252.60	252.30	252.00	+0.30	20,622
286.30	212.00	Apr	256.50	255.30	256.20	+0.30	23,296
293.00	225.00	June	260.70	259.30	260.40	+0.30	20,490
297.50	229.50	Aug	264.80	264.20	264.60	+0.30	13,187
299.30	236.00	Oct	268.60	268.00	268.80	+0.30	3,254
305.20	272.50	Dec	273.30	272.50	273.00	+0.30	1,364

IMM

High	Low	Month	High/Low range			Net change	Open interest
264.00	177.60	June	236.20	234.80	235.50	+0.60	22,657
270.60	181.00	Sept	243.00	240.50	241.70	+0.50	11,424
278.00	183.20	Dec	248.40	246.60	247.80	+0.90	9,908
284.90	210.50	Mar	254.50	253.50	254.10	+1.10	9,131
290.80	226.00	June	260.80	259.80	260.50	+1.10	12,271
299.50	231.70	Sept	267.00	265.60	266.90	+1.10	6,639
306.00	262.50	Dec	273.30	271.80	273.30	+1.10	1,718

Note: All prices are $/troy oz; size of contract on both is 100 troy oz.

gold market is certain: the price will continue to fluctuate just as long as currencies differ in international markets, as long as inflation rates differ between nations and as long as some people think the price of gold is too high while others believe it is too low. I have divided the rest of this chapter into sections covering strategies for bullion, futures trading and options.

Bullion strategies

The first and most obvious strategy involving bullion is simply 'buy and hold'. This may be termed the 'investment' type of risk-taking, where the investor buys a certain amount of bullion (either all at once, or over a period of time on a scaled-up or -down, or dollar-averaging, program), and holds for the future as a hedge against some unforeseen catastrophe to paper money, including dollars. This investor completely disregards gold price fluctuations (except to position more bullion if the price drops) and chances are will never sell the pile of gold involved but rather pass it on to his heirs if the envisaged catastrophe to paper money does not occur during his life.

But there are other types of bullion buyers, including bullion dealers, who are more interested in generating a return on their investment and in arbitrage profits. For example, a bullion trader who was long in 1000 ounces of gold purchased in April, 1979, at $233, could simultaneously, on the New York Comex or the Chicago IMM, go short in (sell) ten lots of gold at prices higher than his cost in April. Consequently if such trading was accomplished he further had the choice of

(a) covering the short sale for profits if the market declines;
(b) delivering his gold for profits if the market either rises or declines;
(c) covering his short at a loss if the market rises and going short again at a higher level while keeping the bullion in storage.

Table 5.1 indicates prices for April 12, 1979, on both the Comex and the IMM. Notice that Comex does not trade September gold whilst IMM does, and that there are variations in the prices of the months concomitantly traded (nearby June Comex closed at $235.60, while nearby June IMM closed at $235.50). Note the 'Open interest' column, the meaning of which is explained further on.

Of course, the owner of the bullion could have sold April,

1980, gold short at $256.20 on Comex and assured an annual return on his pile of about 10%. While such a yield on money is not unusual in the high interest market in the United States or Europe it is still better than that earned in a savings bank or savings and loan association account. Actually, one market-watcher points out that if an investor had bought $1 million worth of gold on December 31, 1974, and had sold it four years after the investment (on December 31, 1978), profit for the four-year period would have been only 14.5% on the invested capital or 3.6% on an annualized basis. The futures markets therefore are customarily used by owners of bullion to presell their bullion at prices that will bring profits or stop losses.

But holders of bullion at times use the futures market to replace bullion sold on the physical marketplaces. For example, the price of gold in London, Zurich or Paris may be higher than the prices on the Comex or IMM for the spot month. In this regard the bullion holder simply sells on the physical market and replaces his or her sale at a lower price by buying on the futures exchanges. Naturally sales of physicals into the London, Paris or Zurich markets would require maintenance of a stockpile of gold in those cities available for ready delivery on a cash basis.

To sum up, then, owners of gold bullion may presell their holdings for profits or losses on futures exchanges, making delivery during the spot month or covering their sales by making offsetting buys and maintaining their gold inventory at desired levels; or, on the other hand, they may actually sell into the physical marketplaces and replace or add to their inventory by purchases made by going long in the spot month in the futures markets.

Of course, owners of gold bullion who realize that the normal futures markets are reflective of a contango (where the nearby months are trading at lower prices than the far-out months because of the cost of carrying the physicals, etc.) can gain an annual return on their stockpile via cash-and-carry transactions. Naturally, when deducting the cost of invested capital and the costs of storage and insurance on the bullion owned, the cash-and-carry at 10% per annum is not at all attractive. But the situation or strategy is there if the holder of the bullion wants to employ it.

It seems to me that if an investor has no desire of becoming a bullion dealer (it takes 2000–4000 ounces to be able to buy at or near the gold fixing in London) he would only accumulate physical gold for posterity, while speculation for the present in gold futures might make the most sense because money can be made whether the price of gold goes up or down. That is why it is time to discuss trading strategies with gold futures.

Gold futures strategies

For simplification purposes we shall assume that the trader will be interested (long or short) in 100 ounce gold futures contracts, although there are contracts that range from one kilogram to 400 ounces if desired. And to keep from referring to more than one exchange, we are going to confine our comments on futures trading strategies to the New York Comex. Of course, what we have to say applies as well to the Chicago IMM, to Winnipeg, the New York Mercantile Exchange and the MidAmerica Exchange.

The first strategy is going long in a future as a substitute for actually owning 100 ounces of gold. Assume for example that a purchase of 100 ounces of bullion at $500 per ounce were contemplated at some time during the spring. This would obviously require a cash outlay (or a cash-and-borrowed-money outlay) of $50,000. Now if the prospective buyer went long in August Comex gold (one contract) at $500 only $6000 would be required as original margin and the balance of the $44,000 could be earning interest in Treasury bills, a savings account, or similar. When August arrived, the holder of the futures contract could 'roll it over' to a farther-out month and keep his foot in the door with bullion while the money that would have normally been locked up in the gold is earning interest and working for the investor every day. Of course, if the price of gold declined while the holder was long in the future he or she might be asked to put up maintenance margin. To do this the holder simply would withdraw the amount needed from the $44,000 cash reserve and when the price of gold rebounded could withdraw equity and have it earning interest again.

In essence, this is the real superiority and beauty of the futures market over the physical market. If you bought 100 ounces of gold bullion and locked up $50,000 for a year or two you would be tying up money that could earn at least $5,500 a year at current interest rates. Moreover, if gold went up in price in the interim, say to $600 an ounce, and you were long in the physicals, the chances are that you would do nothing. But if you were long in the futures, all you would have to do is ask your broker to hand you a check for your equity. Equity is the amount of paper money a position earns over the required margin for the contract. Now if you already have put down $6000 deposit when purchasing the gold contract at $500 and the going price of that future is $600, the broker will hand you a check for $10,000 which you can stick in the bank to earn more money for your account. Incidentally, such money taken from an account is not taxable in the United States—only when the position is liquidated are the profits taxable. Thus, a trader long in a June contract with $10,000 equity above the required deposit can withdraw the funds, put them to work and not be liable for the taxes until the position is liquidated or rolled over. This could have some advantages in tax management, by holding futures positions into the next calendar year and withdrawing the equity to use for this year without paying taxes this year, for instance.

By now you may be quite aware that the holder of a bullion position which has appreciated cannot reap any benefits from it unless either the position is sold for profits or the holder borrows money at high interest rates from a bank or other agency, putting up the gold as collateral. Thus, for investors or traders who want to commit themselves to 100–1000 ounces of gold, the futures markets are far superior to any other medium for taking the risk of being outright long in the metal.

Now let us examine the leverage aspects of being long in 100 ounces of bullion as against being long in a gold futures contract.

To buy 100 ounces of bullion at current prices, about $50,000 would be required. To go long outright in one contract at about the same price only $6000 margin is required. Since the contract is 100 ounces, gold would have to go to $1000 an ounce in order for the holder of the bullion to double his or her money. But the future only has to appreciate $60 an ounce for the contract holder to double his money.

Naturally, if the price drops to $400, the owner of 100 ounces of bullion who has paid $50,000 has a 'paper' loss of $10,000. What has the purchaser of the future obtained in this same instance? Also a loss of $10,000, but the futures holder has been cushioned in the meantime by the interest being earned by the money that would have been locked up in the physical!

The trader in futures, of course, cannot accomplish cash-and-carry maneuvers against a pile of physicals, but that kind of trader can do spreading and *simulate* such a maneuver. For example, the trader could have gone long in December, 1979, Comex gold at $247 and simultaneously have gone short February, 1980, gold at $252/oz. He could have waited for December and actually taken delivery and in turn have delivered in February at the presold higher price, or he could have rolled over his position before December was reached. In addition, some traders utilize *butterfly spreads* in which they may go long in one December contract, go short in two February contracts and go long in one April contract—*all at the same time.* Subsequently they will trade the market by 'lifting' one or more legs (offsetting or closing out one or more positions) and putting on others. What it all amounts to is that spreading—whether in its most simple form (long in one month and short in another month in the same contract on the same exchange), or whether in a more complicated form (long and short on same or differing exchanges in gold contracts varying in number)—is an attempt to profit from price aberrations while being hedged (long and short).

The simplest spread, as just mentioned, is the *intramarket spread,* where the spreader goes long one contract and short another future in the same commodity—in this case gold—in differing months at differing prices. A more complicated spread is the *intermarket spread* where the spreader goes long in one month in one contract market and goes short in the same or another month on another exchange—for example, referring to Table 5.1, going long in one June Comex gold at $235.60 and short one September IMM gold at $241.70.

Because activity in the various months on futures exchanges varies on a daily basis (as for instance in the open positions in Table 5.1) there are opportunities for *arbitrage.* By definition arbitrage is simultaneously buying and selling the same thing in two different market places for a profit. And daily opportunities for such arbitrages crop up on the floor of the futures exchanges. To effect gold arbitrages successfully one would have to be equipped to monitor the quotations on gold exchanges around the world. One would also have to have access to physicals markets as well as futures markets. The successes of Mocatta, J. Aron, Phillip Brothers and other bullion dealers around the world in this connection are of course matters of private information and secrecy, but it is a safe speculation to surmise that much of the flow of gold from the US Treasury and the IMF auctions finds

ready buyers at bullion dealers because of the arbitrage opportunities. I might also go out on a limb and claim that if there were
not gold futures exchanges with ready speculators the monthly
auctions would not find such ready and willing bidders at or near
the London fixings.

Traders who utilize the futures markets in their attempt to
profit from price fluctuations in gold should learn all they can
about the exchanges they intend to trade on and the contract they
intend to participate in. Features of gold futures trading include
price ranges intra-day and for the week, month and life of
contract, open interest size, proximity to the spot market and
delivery terms.

Of course, if the trader never intends to receive or deliver the
physical gold involved in the futures contracts it is not necessary
to cram up on the delivery details and costs. But the chances are
that there may be occasion—especially when it comes to trading
against gold options—where delivery might be required.

I shall now expand on some of the features of the futures
markets mentioned above so that your own trading strategies can
be broadened. Let's start with the price range. Prices for gold
futures change in 'points', with one point the equivalent of one
cent. Thus, if the price of gold advances from $500 to $501 per
ounce during a trading session, it has advanced 100 points, or $1
an ounce, representing an advance of $100 for the contract. If
commissions run $50–$75 for the round turn on a gold futures
trade (depending on where you do your business) then an
advance of at least 50 points would be needed for a trader who is
long to break even, or a decline of at least 50 points for a trader
who is short. It is not at all unusual during a single trading session
for the price of gold futures to advance by $2 an ounce (200 points)
and decline by the same amount before the trading session ends.
That is why there is often the opportunity during a single trading
session for both longs and shorts to make profits—and, of course,
to lose money if their timing is wrong.

Speaking of timing, the strongest markets in the gold pits
usually come at the beginning (opening) of trading in the morning
or the close of trading in the afternoon. The worst time to make
any trades at all (buy or sell) seems to be between the hours of
11.45 a.m. and 1.45 p.m., New York time. In the spring of the
year this is quite strenuous on British-based traders because New
York is six hours behind London. Thus a London gold trader's life
is arduous indeed if one considers a typical trading day.

The trader arrives before the gold fixing at his London office and reviews the Hong Kong and the Paris and Zurich markets. Then the first fixing shortly after 10 a.m. gives direction to what will come later in the States. The market opens in New York at about 9.30 a.m., or 3.30 p.m. London time, giving the trader a chance for a bit of lunch. But the futures markets in the States don't close till after 2.30 p.m. New York time, causing the London trader to miss his or her dinner at 8 p.m. By the time the situation has been reviewed it is after 9 p.m. in London and the trader, to say the least, is both hungry and tired!

Now back at the beginning of this chapter we contended that money could be made attacking the problem of profits in futures from either the long side or the short side. A review of prices and price action of the past clearly reveals that our premise has some foundation. In this regard, of course, charts and charting systems rear their complicated heads—bar charts, point and figure charts and certain systems such as cycles and the Elliot Wave system. Trading from the technical point of view (using chart signals, etc.) is an exercise that assumes all the fundamentals of supply and demand with respect to gold are already in the going price and that the need is to determine the quantity and depth of the immediate marketplace, including how many stop-loss orders to buy and to sell are surrounding the price of the last sale. There are many works published on how to trade from the technical viewpoint and we do not intend to review what is written on that moot subject here. But it is sufficient to remind the reader that trading with charts has become increasingly popular everywhere and short-term price movements in gold as well as in other precious metals traded on futures exchanges are subject to price distortions because of the number of short-term traders who follow similar signals from similar charting systems.

There is also a growing group of contrarians, traders who want to go against the crowd; and these rugged individuals who are determined to trade against the herd pay deep attention to the volume statistics and the open interest. The open interest, for those who may be mystified by the term, is simply the number of contracts that remain to be settled or delivered for any particular contract month. Thus, Table 5.1 indicates that for June Comex gold the open interest was 26,766, meaning that 26,766 contracts were bought and 26,766 contracts were sold but remained unsettled at the time of publication of the open interest figure. The larger the open interest figure, the more liquid the market and the more popular the trading month. In most commodities futures the nearby months generally have larger open interest than the far out months. But in gold, as well as silver, this may not always be true because many traders have positions in spreads which cover both nearby and far-out deliveries.

Incidentally, part of the popularity of gold spreads stems from the reduced margin required for the spreads. While, as we have mentioned, the minimum speculator margin for outright long or short positions in a gold futures contract is $6000, for spreads it is only $500. Moreover, there is much less chance of getting a margin call against outstanding spreads since the months move together generally, while an outright long or short can deteriorate badly in adverse markets.

Now while there is of course risk in going long or short in a gold futures contract, or a gold futures spread (if bullish one buys a spread, if bearish one sells a spread), there is limited risk in the purchase of gold options. Indeed, purchase of a proper gold option could be the most sensible way to go long or short in this volatile market.

Gold options strategies

A call option is a contract made between a buyer and seller (grantor) for which the buyer pays a money fee (premium) for the right to acquire 100 ounces of 995 gold at a set price (the strike price) for a fixed time period (an agreed contract termination or expiration date). The buyer of the call then pays for the right to position 100 ounces of pure gold at a fixed price at his option any time up to and including the expiration date of the call. Obviously, if the price of gold declines during the term of the call, the buyer will lose his or her money premium. *But that is all that can be lost.* Conversely, if the price of gold rises during the term of the option the holder or buyer can follow one of several strategies:

1. Resell the call contract for value.
2. Go short 100 ounces of gold in the futures market against the option.
3. Hold on to the option and exercise it (declare it) on or before expiration date and receive delivery of the gold bullion involved.

A put, by definition, is simply the opposite of a call in that the purchaser of a put on 100 ounces of gold at a set strike price pays a premium for the right to sell to or deliver to the endorser of the put contract the 100 ounces of 995 gold at the agreed price at any time at the holder's option up to and including the expiration date.

It becomes obvious, then, that the purchase of a put limits the risk of a trader who is bearish on gold and decides to go short in the market. If the trader buys a gold put, then the most he can lose if wrong is the cost (premium) involved. Moreover, since the trader by purchasing a put has in effect 'presold' 100 ounces of gold at the contract price, he can trade the futures market or the bullion market from the long side with each 100 ounces involved completely protected against downside erosion by the presence of the puts.

In similar manner, a trader can purchase gold calls and go short in the futures markets, all the while completely protected against upside erosion of the short position by the presence of the gold calls in portfolio.

If options are so good, therefore, why doesn't everybody use them? In the first place, the number of bona fide sources offering gold puts and gold calls can be counted on the fingers of one hand. In the second place, traders have an aversion to paying for protection, because gold options cost money and unless they are sensibly used may prove to be unwarranted expenses in quiet markets. But in volatile markets, puts and calls are something else!

In markets that move sharply up and down, similar to those we have experienced in gold since November 1978, properly employed gold puts and calls and concomitant opposite action in the futures markets can create fantastic protected profits. In this regard, the following is a listing of some of the uses of gold puts and gold calls:

1. *Calls for limited-risk approach to the bull-side of the market.* Instead of buying bullion or futures, buy a call for every 100 ounces desired. If the market rises, the call can be resold for profits, or futures can be shorted for profits, or bullion can be acquired below market via exercise.
2. *Calls for protection on the short-side of the market.* Instead of going short in the futures market and inserting protective buy-stop-loss orders, it makes more sense to first go long in gold calls and then short in the future on the rise. When the price of

the future drops, cover and recoup part of the premium and then go short on the rise again—all the while limiting possible loss to the cost of the calls.

3. *Puts for limited-risk approach to the bear-side of the market.* Instead of going outright short in the futures, buy a put for every 100 ounces desired short. If market drops, puts can be resold for profits, or futures can be positioned on the long side and sold on the rise, or bullion can be purchased in a declining gold market completely protected by the puts and if the market does not rally before the expiration of the puts the bullion can be actually delivered at the higher-than-market put strike price.

4. *Puts for protection on the long-side of the market.* Instead of going long in gold futures and exposing oneself to the risks of a down market, purchase a put for every 100 ounces bought in the futures or bullion market. If the price of gold rises, the futures or bullion can be resold for profits, but if the price falls, the most that can be lost are the monies involved in the purchase of the puts, plus, of course, any commissions or charges relating to the long bullion or futures contracts protected by the puts.

At the time of writing there are probably only two bona fide option contracts offered to sensible speculators who seek the kind of protection options offer. These are the Mocatta Options and the Valeurs-White Weld Options. Valeurs has been found acceptable for distribution to Americans but currently still has not filed the necessary papers for final Commodity Futures Trading Commission endorsement. The chances are, however, that they will be filed by the time this book is published. Valeurs only vends gold calls, not puts, but Mocatta offers through accepted dealers both puts and calls on gold. Their option covers 100 ounces of gold bullion 995, and of course Comex and IMM deliverable grade gold.

Quotes for Mocatta options are available on the Reuters Monitor and are published in trade papers such as the *American Metal Market* and the *Journal of Commerce*. The published quotes, of course, are subject to change, with the premiums for calls rising as the price of gold futures on the IMM rise and the premiums for puts declining at the same time. (Conversely, the premiums for the calls will decline and the premiums for the puts will rise in a falling gold futures market.) In addition to the premiums, since Mocatta does not deal directly with the public, agents who distribute Mocatta options add on their commission or fee. Thus, if a June $500 gold call covering 100 ounces is offered by Mocatta at $5000, the prospective purchaser will have to pay an additional sum of money for the option as follows:

ContiCommodity Services	$100 over premium
Bache, Halsey Stuart	5% of the premium added
Shearson, Loeb Rhoades	5% of the premium added
ITG	$1/7$th of the premium added

It is immediately obvious from the above that if the option premium exceeds $2000, ContiCommodity's fee will be the cheapest; the average premium runs at $2000–$4000. For more details of Mocatta gold options see Appendix C.

In the case of Valeurs calls, Conti charged only $50 per call over the five kilogram (161 ounce) option before the ban of June 1, 1978, and will probably resume selling at that modest fee rate when Valeurs becomes acceptable to the CFTC.

In the meantime we look forward eagerly to the time when the Comex, the IMM and the New York Mercantile Exchange will be able to have gold options traded in their rings so that speculators who seek the limited-risk protection provided by bona fide gold options will be able to purchase them with only the customary $50–$75 per contract round-turn commission. Winnipeg Exchange began to trade gold options in late spring 1979, and fuller details of this can be found in Appendix D. However, the volume of trading there is insignificant compared to the potential volume of the major exchanges already mentioned. The début of trading gold options on the major exchanges will herald opportunities for people already long in bullion to grant (sell) gold calls and thus earn 25% or more a year on their gold piles. In addition, the introduction of listed puts will provide speculators with the chance of earning premiums by granting puts in a rising market and granting calls in a falling market against a money deposit. In every case the grantor of a put would be better off than a buyer of bullion because he would automatically buy the bullion cheaper by virtue of the premium received for the sale of the put. And the grantor of the call would have presold gold already owned at a higher-than-market level by virtue of the premium received for the gold calls granted.

Obviously, a book could be written devoted just to the strategies of trading in exchange options on gold, silver, platinum and other commodities. When these options are approved by the CFTC for exchange trading I will probably write such a book, Lord willing, but right now it is sufficient to state that options such as the Mocatta ones can be used greatly to advantage by traders willing to learn about them and willing to realize that Mocatta makes a two-way market and the price of gold does not have to move up to the strike price of an away-from-the-market option in order for the holder to profit. (Mocatta has published literature on this subject, which is available to readers who write for it.)

6

Gold hedging strategies

Hedging was briefly touched on in Chapter 4, but it is important enough to warrant fuller treatment here. People who deal in gold can lose plenty of money through price changes.

Buying hedges

Let us begin with our previous example of the manufacturer of gold jewelry. He buys gold in sheet form and stamps his adornments from it, sending his salespeople out into the field in the spring of each year to take orders for delivery of finished goods to stores for the Christmas season. The offering price for these golden trinkets has been calculated not only on the cost of labor and sales commissions and of shipping, packing and so forth, but also by the estimated cost of the raw material—in this case, a form of gold of the purity required to make the articles. (For readers quite unfamiliar with the gold trade, it should be pointed out that gold is sold in many forms, such as alloys, rods, bars, tubing, wire, leaf, foil, powder, salts, ingots and stampings.)

To assure himself of a ready supply of the kind of gold he needs at a price commensurate with the price of the finished goods being offered, the jewelry manufacturer has to hedge. By putting on a hedge in this case, he would have to be assured of a supply sufficient for his needs, deliverable at the time required, and within the price range anticipated. He can readily accomplish this by contracting with a supplier of the forms needed for delivery forward. He can prepay the entire lot of gold involved, or leave a deposit and pay the rest on delivery, or, if he has previously done business of a substantial nature with the supplier, simply send a purchase order with delivery and price instructions.

But such a trade would be fine for a commodity whose price is reasonably stable. By now it is readily apparent that the price of gold will, if anything, continue to fluctuate as long as it is considered a commodity and not sold at a fixed price as part of the monetary system, as it was prior to the Bretton Woods Agreement cancellation. Therefore, there is a very good chance that any forward contract made between the supplier and the user would be escalated by whatever amount gold may have risen in the interim between the purchase order and the delivery date. In this regard, of course, the jeweler may have taken orders for the finished goods from distributors with the proviso that, if the price of gold rises before their orders are delivered, such a rise will be reflected in their costs.

Since the jewelry manufacturer is interested in turnover with profits and seeks constantly to keep the goodwill of his clients, he actually can effect a buying hedge in the futures markets and thereby *guarantee* that his customers will receive delivery of the vended merchandise at the price at which the order was taken, even if the price of gold soars. The buy hedge in the futures market, of course, is for price protection purposes only and the chances are that the hedger will never take delivery of the gold contracts but will liquidate them at the same time as his actual purchase of the required gold forms in the cash market.

The following specific example will illustrate this in more detail. The XYZ Jewelry Company needs 1000 ounces of gold in stampings form of 18K purity and would be charged by their supplier at the rate of $520 per ounce deliverable in December if the order were placed during the preceding March. Having given his supplier just such an order the astute hedger would simultaneously go long in ten December Comex contracts at, say, about $500 per ounce. When November arrives, if the price of gold has risen to, say, $530 per ounce for the December contract, the hedger will probably have to pay his supplier at least $540 per ounce for the stampings. So he pays $30 an ounce *higher* than he would have done had he actually purchased the gold forms back in March in the spot market, and offsets his obvious loss with the $30 per ounce profit from liquidating his long futures position.

Now assume the price of gold had not risen but instead had fallen from $500 to $470 an ounce for the Comex December futures: then the user would probably have been able to buy his gold forms in the cash market at least $30 an ounce less than the price the previous March, but the benefits from the cheaper cash purchase would, of course, have been offset by the $30 an ounce loss to the futures position upon liquidation.

So, if making a buying hedge in the futures market offers complete price protection in volatile commodities, why doesn't every user do it?

The answers to this rather simple-sounding question are many and possibly involved. But what it boils down to is that managers of inventory really don't want only protection: they want profits. In other words, they generally are uninterested in the kind of hedge that simply assures them material at a predetermined price. What they really seem to want is either a hedging medium that can not only protect them but also provide profits along with said protection.

Remarkable as it may seem, only options can provide this circumstance. To explain, let's return to the jewelry manufacturer. If instead of going long in ten December Comex contracts he had purchased five Mocatta December gold calls (200 ounces for each call), and had included the cost of his premiums in the selling price of the finished goods, this is what would have happened, no matter which way the market in gold went after the calls were purchased:

1. If the market price of bullion had soared, the holder of the options could have resold them for profits which would have offset his increased cost in the cash markets.
2. If the price of gold had plummeted, the hedger would have lost the money on the calls, but would have *profited* by being able to purchase his gold forms at a much lower than antici-pated price in the cash markets.

It naturally follows that if the hedger seeks only price protection he can have it by making buy hedges in the futures markets and cash purchases at the time the materials are needed in the cash markets; while the hedger who seeks protection and possible profits must do his buy hedging with gold calls purchased from Mocatta, Valeurs or any other bona fide source. The debut of listed options at some future date in America will greatly reduce the cost of gold option premiums as competition in a free market replaces the present monopolistic dealer market.

Selling hedges

The second major hedging strategy, of course, is the selling hedge. This is often utilized by stockpilers and bullion dealers in order to assure a fair price for the sale of either inventory on hand, or inventory to be positioned. For example, during Janaury, 1980, the price of gold had surged to an all-time record fixing of $854 per ounce. At that time bullion dealers and possessors of gold stocks (e.g. gold miners) could have 'presold' their inventory, or part of it, via the futures market in the form of a selling hedge. Thus, a supplier of gold forms who may have been carrying the equivalent of 25,000 ounces of pure gold in stock could have gone short in 250 contracts of May gold at say $875 in January and covered at under $500. The $375 per ounce profit in the futures market would have cushioned the decline in price of the materials held on hand which would necessarily have to be sold at a cheaper price in May than the materials would have brought during February. The sell-hedge was created to cushion the inventory holder during price declines.

But what if the price of gold instead of dropping by May had soared from $875 to say $1000? Then the hedger would have lost $125 per ounce by covering his abortive short sale and, of course, would have made up that loss by selling his inventory on the cash market at higher than February prices.

So, again, if a sell hedge is so good, why doesn't everybody who owns a substantial amount of gold take advantage of it? Here again, the sentiment seems to be that people—even sensible business people—don't want mere protection. They want also a chance to profit. The purchase of gold puts is the only way such profits might be achieved.

For example, our gold forms supplier mentioned above could have purchased 250 Mocatta gold May puts (covering 25,000 ounces) and would have *insured* his merchandise to any downside risk limited to the cost of the puts, if the gold market had declined. But what if the gold market had soared? The premiums expended for such 'insurance' in the form of puts would be lost, but the merchandise which had been protected on the downside in case of a decline could bring non-locked-in profits on the upside in a soaring gold market.

There we have it: the words 'locked in.' People, in my experience over the past forty years, shy away from situations where the protection locks them in, as it would do if they resorted to the futures markets for either a buy hedge or a sell hedge. But options not only provide the needed protection, they also leave the door open to profits. It is a practical certainty that when gold options (puts and calls) are listed for trading on North American commodity exchanges their popularity as hedging media which allow for profits to the hedger will, to say the least, burgeon. In April 1979 listed gold call options began trading on the Winnipeg Exchange. A summary of the rules is to be found in Appendix D. At the time of writing, US commission merchants cannot vend Winnipeg options to the American public, but naturally brokers abroad or outside the United States can.

7

Gold trading mechanics

Bullion trading

Happily, the trader in precious metals, including gold, does not have to busy himself or herself looking for the bullion. It is readily available—and saleable—all over the world. But the big questions that have to be answered when it comes to purchase of physicals are:

(a) Is it intended to take possession of the gold?
(b) What are the costs involved of purchase, storage, insurance and eventual sales?
(c) How sound is the firm selling the gold?
(d) Most importantly, what is the reputation of the firm offering it?

I have already stated my preference for never touching, seeing, handling, or hefting any gold or gold coins that I might be inclined to position for trading purposes. But some readers may desire receipt of the bullion they buy or the coins they amass. In this regard, both bullion and coins can be shipped to purchasers from any country in the world and to any country in the world via air express, or ship delivery. Customarily, in cases that do not involve smuggling of course, the gold is shipped insured and eventually delivered to the receiving bank or destination by bonded messenger.

All this incurs various charges and the purchaser is advised to check the charges before any bullion or coins are positioned with a view of receipt and delivery. Primarily, gold is vended to the retail purchaser via a chain. The gold will come from the producer through the bullion broker to authorized agents and retailed by said agents to the public everywhere.

Obviously, bullion brokers such as Mocatta, J. Aron and Phillips Brothers (Engelhard Minerals) normally do not do any business except with large commercial accounts and authorized agents. These agents may be coin stores, banks, brokerage firms who are members of various exchanges, and some money-changing firms such as Deak, Perrera or Manfred Tortella & Brooks.

The situation for bullion purchasers in the United States is slightly different from that for purchasers on the Continent. For example, in Switzerland it is customary to buy gold from the Swiss Bank, Crédit-Suisse, Union Bank, etc., rather than from agents or dealers. In West Germany and France the same conditions exist—purchasers in order to be sure of authenticity and weights do their buying from banks.

In the United States, on the other hand, most of the gold vended to prospective buyers comes from authorized agents of the bullion dealers. It is true, of course, that the Republic National Bank in New York is one of the three authorized distributors of Krugerrands (Mocatta and J. Aron are the other two) and that gold bullion and coins can be purchased through that bank and through the Swiss Bank too. But the lion's share of retail gold business in America comes from purchases made through coin dealers, brokerage firms and other authorized agents.

Since there have been abuses in the past and probably will be in the future by sources who claim they are agents of bullion dealers, it is sensible to make sure of the relationship before forwarding any funds for bullion or coins to be delivered later. In the way of sincere advice we offer the following list of 'don'ts' in such dealings:

1. Don't buy anything from any firm that calls on the telephone. Reliable sources don't have to solicit via the phone.
2. Don't buy anything by mail from any firm offering wares that contain gold or silver bullion on the basis that those objects will become more valuable due to the increase in value of the metal content over the years.
3. Don't take any agents' word that they are 'authorized' representatives of Mocatta, or J. Aron or any other reliable bullion source. It only takes a phone call or letter to find out the facts.

4. Don't buy any bullion before ascertaining the costs of annual
storage and insurance and, if contemplating delivery, determine in advance what delivery charges will entail.

Certain American members of the New York Stock Exchange
have facilities to buy gold bullion for customers (Bache Halsey
Stuart even casts its own 10 ounce gold ingots). Such firms as
Bache, Merrill Lynch, Thomson McKinnon and Shearson Loeb
Rhoades maintain 'departments', and have personnel assigned,
to handle the gold-buying needs of their customers. As a general
rule, to make sure you will receive proper treatment and authen-
tic gold, whether asking for delivery or leaving the bullion in
storage, it makes sense to deal with a firm that is a member of a
major stock or commodity exchange. The larger the firm and the
more memberships it holds, naturally the more sound and reliable the firm could be (when it comes to complaints, at any rate).
But even small firms that hold exchange memberships are more
likely to offer legitimate service than a firm with a decorative
name that has a post office box and a desk in an office building
somewhere and little else in the way of assets.

Futures trading

Gold futures are traded mainly in North America and the bulk of
the activity is concentrated in New York and Chicago. Since these
trading centers handle the greatest number of trades and have the
largest outstanding open positions, it is sensible to concentrate on
them in our examination of the mechanics of trading gold futures.

In Chicago, gold futures of 100 ounces each are traded on both
the Chicago Board of Trade (CBOT) and the Chicago Mercantile
International Monetary Market (IMM). The CBOT originally
started with a three kilogram gold contract but eventually found
that because of American aversion to metrics people would rather
trade 100 ounce contracts than a metric amount approximating to
the same thing. As a result, the Chicago IMM, bolstered by broad
advertising campaigns, rapidly became the principal arena for
gold trading in that city.

In New York City, two exchanges also were involved in the
start of gold futures trading on the last day of 1974—the New
York Mercantile Exchange and the Comex.

As in the case of the CBOT, the contract on the New York
Mercantile was in metric form (one kilogram) while the contract

on the Comex was for 100 ounces. The result was that a trader had to buy three 'Merc' contracts to receive almost the equivalent of one Comex contract and would have had to pay three commissions as compared to only one. This, of course, helped the Comex and hurt the other exchange, so that it wasn't long before the Comex became the leading gold futures trading arena in New York.

To trade in futures the participant must be aware that there are both margins and commissions involved. In the case of the 100 ounce gold contract on, say, the Comex, $6000 is the required exchange margin at the time of writing. But the futures commission merchant who is servicing your account may require more than the exchange margin—say, $1000 a contract. In this case the margin is called 'house margin'. Since all margins on futures contracts are simply deposits of good faith against contracts that they be either eventually fulfilled or offset by effecting opposite transactions in the same contract month, they are simply 'binders' on the original contracts. If the price of the future drops, in the case of customers who are 'long' (holders of contracts) the exchange and the broker demand maintenance margin from the clients (see chapter 4). If the price of the underlying futures recovers, then the maintenance margin may be withdrawn from the equity.

The word 'equity' assumes vital importance to both the trader and his broker, since:

1. If the equity falls, the broker has to ask for more margin and may be in jeopardy if the customers don't supply it on demand; and the customer has to come up with more money.
2. On the other hand, should the customers account *improve* in equity (long positions rise in value and short positions improve because of a decline in futures values, etc.) then this rise in equity generates an increase in purchasing power (excess) which the broker receives from the clearing house and applies to the customers' accounts; the customer can either withdraw the actual excess funds or buy more contracts.

An example of this situation is the following hypothetical case. In the third week of April, 1980, a customer decided June Comex gold at $547 was a good risk for a trading turn and went long in ten contracts at that level. A week or so later gold moved up and

June gold traded at $567 per ounce. What was the customer's situation?

Bought ten Comex June gold contracts (100 ounces each) at $547 per ounce.
Deposited initial margin at $6000 per contract: $60,000 total.
Gold moved to $557, or by $20 per ounce, a gain of $20,000 on the 1000 ounces involved.
Customer now had equity of his original $60,000, plus the $20,000 generated by the market movement in the futures.
Customer could withdraw $20,000 and use it elsewhere or go long in up to three more contracts of June gold (or any other month).

Of course, if gold had dropped $20 an ounce to trade at $527 instead of $567, much of the customer's equity would have been wiped out and he would have had to supply maintenance margin to bring the account up to the proper equity level.

It is on such foundations that fortunes in the futures markets are made and lost. The management of equity is perhaps the real key to riches or disaster, depending on how much money the trader has available. Obviously, had the trader in our foregoing example put on ten more contracts at $567, he would have been long in twenty contracts at an average price of $557 and every dollar move up or down would have changed his equity by $2000, and a $30 move would have either doubled his equity or wiped it out, depending on the direction of the move.

But the trader who eyes the futures markets as a means of making a living, like the subsistence gambler who picks off the win or lose bar at the dice game enough to come back another day, normally doesn't wait for such large moves. Instead, the 'scalper' seems content to enter the market during a rising or falling intraday trend and get out of his position the same day, or within the next day or two, with small profits. The old stock market cliché 'You can't get hurt taking small profits' has evidently influenced many scalpers who can enter the market and exit very quickly, making or losing a relatively small amount of money. There is a great deal going for such a trading approach, most of all the fact that day trading requires no margins.

To explain this approach, let us take a further example. Assume a trader has an open account at a futures commission merchant (FCM) and goes long in one June Comex gold at $557 on a sunny day in May. That morning, after the opening, gold moves up 100 points ($1 an ounce). The trader figures an intraday movement has started and buys twenty more contracts at $558. An hour or so later, June gold stands at $560—up 300 points on the day and up 200 points from where the trader 'pyramided' (added the ten contracts at $558 to the existing one at $557). Further assume that the trader is nervous about a setback and immediately liquidates the twenty contracts bought at $558 for the $560 price, winding up the session still long in the original contract purchased at $557. How does he stand? And how much margin did he have to put up for the eleven contracts long?

In the first place he doesn't have to put up *any margin at all* for the twenty contracts bought and sold during the day (see Glossary, under 'Day trade'). Since he grossed 200 points on 2000 ounces, his closed-out profit was—even after commissions of, say, $250 (and day-trade commissions are usually only half the overnight rate)—a good return on the $6000 margin required for the single contract left in the account overnight at a basis of $557. And so this kind of trading, which occurs every single day in and around the gold pits in Chicago and New York, adds the speculative flavor and spice to the marketplace. An in-and-out trader who is conservative and nimble can earn $500–$1000 or more a day simply trading the intraday gold trend. Of course, the trader will not be successful all the time, but as long as he or she can glean or scalp profits consistently (60% of the time) the exercise is both fruitful and exciting.

A final note on margins and day trading: if, in the United States stock markets, a trader went long in 3000 shares of IBM at $60 a share and sold out the same day at $62, he would have grossed $6000 before commissions. But to earn that money and not be in violation of the Federal Reserve Board margin laws, he would have had to deposit the $180,000 involved in the purchase of the 3000 IBM shares before being entitled to receive the rewards of his risk in the market. Fortunately, the regulations of futures market trading are a bit more enlightened and no margin money goes to the clearing house of the involved exchange until the positions at the end of the trading session are posted. In the case above of the daring gold speculator who went long in one June gold at $557 and then added twenty more contracts at $558, only to liquidate the twenty at $560, remaining with the single contract started with, the only margin money required to be sent over to the exchange at the commencement of the next morning would have

been the margin for the open and outstanding single long position at $557 which had been in the account overnight, and
nothing at all would have been required for the added longs that
were offset during the trading session.

In addition to scalping operations, futures markets are more
favorable for Americans seeking capital gains of a long-term
nature than stock markets, because the holding period required
for a position to become 'long term' in the futures markets is six
months, while with stock transactions the holding period is
currently one year. And so we do have many holders of precious
metal futures who are currently sitting on some nice long-term
capital gains. This type of trader cannot go in and out quickly, like
the scalper. Instead, he eyes the market from its long-term
possibilities. In this regard it is fitting to now examine what
factors influence the prices of gold in the marketplaces and where
the price is going in the future. To do this we turn to the greatly
belabored term 'gold research'.

8

Gold research

Webster's Dictionary defines 'research' as 'careful or diligent search' and 'studious inquiry or examination'. For the gold trader all the research he and so many others conduct is slanted to answer the question 'Where will the price of gold go?' And if such a rather simple-sounding question can be correctly answered, the researcher further wants to know in what time-frame the price movement will occur.

When conducting do-it-yourself gold research you must be constantly aware of what the precise applications of the work will entail. Obviously, one could spend almost an entire lifetime studying the fundamental aspects of the gold scene—by fundamental I mean the supply/demand picture of the physical metal. On the other hand, the trader may be more interested in the supply/demand of buy and sell orders appearing in the pits on the futures exchanges. Other traders, again, may disregard volume, open interest and the fundamental aspects of supply/demand and instead concern themselves with chart patterns involving point-and-figure formations, box count, price projection and so on. Of course, the technically oriented trader who relies on charts and their patterns, price cycles, etc., may be affluent enough to examine price patterns on a computer and thus attempt projection of where the price of gold is going via the use of linear regression equations and the like.

Thus, gold research from the point of view of a trader normally falls into three distinct but often intertwined varieties:

1. *Fundamental* The supply, demand, production and consumption of the physical metal are intensely inspected and conclu-

sions are drawn as to future supply/demand relationships and the factors that will influence the price of gold at some future time.

2. *Technical*   This involves chart systems—either bar chart or point and figure—whose patterns, subject to the ability of the trader to interpret and project them correctly, will guide him in making market decisions according to certain buy and sell signals provided by the charts.

3. *Statistical*   This involves computerized programs formed from linear regression equations whose parameters can be manipulated and changed by the trader and whose projections may or may not be any more accurate than the signals acted on by the technician.

Fundamental research

Since most people are intelligent enough to realize that there are indeed factors which influence the market price of any commodity, including gold, it will pay to spend some time expanding on this aspect.

By my definition, fundamental research entails the study of the physical metal from the standpoint of how much is available each year for consumers (supply) and how much is actually used by the consumers (demand). If the supply exceeds anticipated demand, then it is logical to assume the price will drop. If demand will exceed the anticipated supply it naturally follows that the market price of the metal should rise.

But how does a trader without a research staff keep track of the gold fundamentals? The answer is either to do business with a giant commodity firm that has a fundamental research department and employs analysts to keep track of the gold fundamentals, or to do it yourself with the help of the United States Department of the Interior.

In the first instance, most of the large commodity firms employ analysts to follow the precious metals as a group, or in the case of firms like Conti have analysts assigned only to gold, or to gold and silver.

In the second instance, the United States Department of Interior, Bureau of Mines, keeps track of the fundamentals on gold production and consumption inside the United States and also around the world. Fig. 8.1 shows a typical gold section in the Bureau's *Mineral Commodity Summaries,* an annual publication issued in monthly sections.

However, the single most impelling fundamental factor involving the price of gold has not been the supply/demand equation, but rather the attitude of the United States toward the metal as a reserve for paper money.

Gold has always been respected around the world as a storehouse of value and traditionally has been used as a reserve by governments against the paper money in circulation. For example, in 1896 there was about $24 in paper outstanding for every gold dollar in the United States Treasury. But in 1980 there was about $17,000 in paper circulating for every dollar's worth of gold in the Treasury. And the attitude of each American Administration from the time of President Eisenhower has been to demonetize the role of gold. This attitude has caused the US Government to dispose of some of its gold holdings at ludicrously cheap prices and the US Government auctions were the most important single influence on the price of the metal until they were halted in November, 1979.

In October, 1978, when President Carter announced the massive monetary intervention to 'rescue' the dollar and the size of the monthly auction was hiked to 1.5 million ounces, the price of gold dropped subsequently to the $193 level. As inflation continued in the United States and it became obvious that the dollar would be stabilised artificially, so that the world would have a 'stable' reserve currency while prices would soar to adjust against the ravages of increasing inflation, the price of gold at the London daily fixings began to recover. Then in the spring of 1979, after the Administration announced a cutback of the size of the monthly auction to 750,000 ounces, gold leaped to a then record fixing of $270.50 per ounce.

It is my personal view that the supply/demand picture in gold will be just about in balance, no matter how much the demand increases, because of fears instilled in the minds and hearts of Americans by uncontrollable inflation. And I also believe that gold as a store of wealth and as an item of value to back up paper money will some day be reinstalled in its rightful place. Hints of this return were reflected in the formation in 1979 of the European Monetary System, which is a pool of paper money backed by 20% in gold deposits of the member countries. But the reestablishment of gold as a reserve for paper money, alas, is still a long way off; in the meantime, the auctions of the United States (if resumed) and the IMF could continue to dominate the price picture. Table 8.1 is a listing of the various auctions held by both

62   <u>GOLD</u>
                        (Data in million troy ounces of metal, unless noted)

1. <u>Domestic Production and Use</u>: The domestic mining industry consists of about 175 mines, nearly all in Western States; more than a third of these produce gold as a principal product. In 1979, 25 mines yielded 95% of the gold produced, and 3 of these accounted for 65%. About 40% of domestic gold is a byproduct of base metal mining, chiefly copper mining. The value of 1979 mine production was about $275 million. Commercial-grade refined gold came from 37 producers; the number of fabricators is about 3,500. Nearly all jewelry manufacturing is centered in the New York City and Providence, R.I., areas. Estimated uses in 1979: Jewelry and arts, 58%, industrial (mainly electronic), 28%, dental, 13%, small bars, etc., mainly for investment, 1%.

2. <u>Salient Statistics--United States</u>:

	1975	1976	1977	1978	1979 e/
Production: Mine	1.05	1.05	1.10	1.00	0.91
Refinery: New (domestic)	1.09	0.95	0.96	1.03	0.80
Secondary (incl. toll)	2.70	2.50	2.45	3.09	3.21
Imports 1/ 2/ 3/	2.66	2.66	4.45	4.69	3.90
Exports 2/	2.69	2.88	7.01	5.51	15.62
Consumption, reported	3.99	4.65	4.86	4.74	5.00
Consumption, apparent	4.54	5.29	5.30	5.10	5.76
Price, average selling: Dollars per ounce	161.49	125.32	148.31	193.55	304.00
Stocks, yearend: Treasury 4/	274.73	274.70	277.57	276.43	263.19
Stocks, yearend: Industry	0.79	0.93	1.98	1.67	0.90
Stocks, yearend: Assigned to futures trading	0.55	0.32	1.84	2.75	2.40
Employment: Mine and mill e/	3,000	3,200	3,200	3,200	3,200
Net import reliance 5/ as a percent of apparent consumption	52	60	61	53	56

3. <u>Recycling</u>: Of an estimated 3.2 million ounces of gold reclaimed from scrap in 1979, about 1.6 million ounces was from old scrap. The balance was from prompt industrial scrap, partly toll-refined. Old scrap supplied about 32% of total gold consumed.

4. <u>Import Sources (1975-78)</u>: Canada 43%, U.S.S.R. 20%, Switzerland 17% (mostly Republic of South African origin), Other 20%. 2/

5. <u>Tariff</u>: No U.S. duties are imposed on imports of unrefined gold or bullion. Ad valorem duties on important items are as follows.

Item	Number	Most Favored Nation (MFN)		Non-MFN
		1/1/80	1/1/87	1/1/80
Plat. or silver-plated	605.27	14.9%	7.5%	65%
Unwrought or semimfd.	605.28	18.5%	8.2%	65%
Rolled	605.60 & 605.66	11.3% & 20%	6.5% & 20%	30% & 65%
Compounds	418.80	5%	5%	25%

6. <u>Depletion Allowance</u>: 15% (Domestic), 14% (Foreign).

e/ Estimate. 1/ General imports through 1978; imports for consumption in 1979.
2/ Excludes official monetary gold movements; also excludes estimates of imported gold coin containing, in million ounces, 1.7 (1975), 1.3 (1976), 1.6 (1977), 3.7 (1978), and 3.8 (1979).
3/ Excludes net bullion flow to market from foreign stocks at the New York Federal Reserve Bank in million ounces: 0.6 (1975), 2.1 (1976), 6.6 (1977), 1.6 (1978), and 0.3 (estimated 1979); from sales of Treasury Department stocks, 1.3 (1975), 2.6 (1978), and 13.5 (estimated 1979); from sales of International Monetary Fund stocks, 3.9 (1976), 4.5 (1977), 3.9 (1978), and 4.1 (estimated 1979).
4/ Includes gold in Exchange Stabilization Fund. Stocks were valued in billion dollars at 11.60 (1975-76), 11.72 (1977), 11.67 (1978), and 11.11 (estimated 1979).
5/ Net import reliance = imports - exports + adjustments for Government and industry stock changes.

Prepared by W. C. Butterman, telephone (202) 634-1071.

Fig. 8.1 Section on gold in *Mineral Commodity Summaries*, January 1980 (reproduced by permission of US Department of the Interior, Bureau of Mines)

7. <u>Government Programs</u>: Monthly public sales of bullion by the Department of the Treasury, begun May 1978, add several million ounces of gold annually to the international market. The Bureau of Mines researches methods of recovering gold and other precious metals from ores and scrap. Improvements are being made in heap-leaching of gold ores using cyanide solutions and in extraction of gold from solutions using activated charcoal. Amenability tests are made on samples from promising gold deposits.

8. <u>Events, Trends, and Issues</u>: As the price of gold continued to climb for the third consecutive year, much exploration activity was reported in the Western States and several new but relatively small mines, were being readied for production. The production of gold, however, declined about 9%, as producers took advantage of the higher gold prices to mine leaner ores.

The New York (Engelhard) daily gold price began the year at $227.10 per troy ounce, fell to the year's low of $217.90 on January 12, and then trended upward for 9 months, rising especially fast in September. After leveling off in October and November, the price again rose in the last days of November, and by December 3 had reached $429.10.

The U.S. Department of the Treasury continued the monthly bullion sales it began in May 1978, offering 1.5 million ounces per month for the first 4 months of the year and 0.75 million ounces per month for the following 6 months. Thereafter, Treasury varied the size and timing of the sales, selling 1.25 million ounces on November 1. Total sales for the year were 11.75 million ounces. Much of the bullion was purchased by European banks and exported from the United States. In June, the International Monetary Fund (IMF) reduced the amount offered at its monthly bullion auctions from 470,000 ounces to 444,000 ounces, and stopped selling gold on a noncompetitive basis to member countries. IMF sales for the year totaled 5.46 million ounces, of which 4.10 million ounces were delivered in the United States. The U.S. futures market remained strong in 1979, and volume traded reached a billion ounces for the year.

U.S. consumption of gold in 1979 increased 5% from 1978. From a 1978 base, demand for gold is expected to increase at an annual rate of 3.2% through 1985.

Environmental pollution control continued to concern domestic gold miners, especially in Alaska, where there are many small placer mines.

9. <u>World Mine Production and Reserve Base</u>:

	Mine Production		Reserve Base*
	1978	1979 e/	
United States	1.0	0.91	45
Canada	1.7	1.7	20
South Africa, Republic of	22.7	23.4	225
Other Market Economy Countries	5.9	6.1	80
Central Economy Countries	8.5	8.8	160
World Total	39.8	40.9	530

In addition to mine resources, the world's above-ground stocks total at least 1.8 billion ounces, of which 1.2 billion ounces are official stocks of the market economy countries, and 0.5 billion ounces are privately held.

10. <u>World Resources</u>: World resources of gold are estimated at 1.9 billion ounces, of which 15% to 20% are byproduct resources. The Republic of South Africa has about half of world resources, the U.S.S.R. about 15%, and the United States about 13%. Most of the 0.25 billion ounce U.S. resource occurs as a byproduct.

11. <u>Substitutes and Alternates</u>: Base metals clad with gold alloys are being used increasingly in electrical/electronic products to economize on gold. Generally, palladium, platinum, and silver may substitute for gold.

* See page 188 for definition.

January 1980

Fig. 8.1 (cont'd)

Gold research

Table 8.1 IMF and US Treasury gold auctions, 1976–1980

IMF

Date	Ounces sold Competitive	Non-comp.	Avg. price per ounce
June 2, 1976	780,000	—	$126.00
July 14, 1976	780,000	—	122.05
Sept 15, 1976	780,000	—	109.40
Oct 27, 1976	779,200	—	117.71
Dec 8, 1976	780,000	—	137.00
Jan 26, 1977	780,000	—	133.26
Mar 2, 1977	524,400	—	146.51
Apr 6, 1977	524,800	—	149.18
May 4, 1977	524,800	—	148.02
June 1, 1977	524,800	—	143.32
July 6, 1977	524,800	—	140.26
Aug 3, 1977	524,800	—	146.26
Sept 7, 1977	524,800	—	147.78
Oct 5, 1977	524,800	—	155.14
Nov 2, 1977	524,800	—	161.86
Dec 7, 1977	524,800	—	160.03
Jan 4, 1978	524,800	—	171.26
Feb 1, 1978	524,800	—	175.00
Mar 1, 1978	524,800	—	181.95
Apr 5, 1978	524,800	—	177.92
May 3, 1978	524,800	—	170.40
June 7, 1978	470,000	925,000	183.09
July 5, 1978	470,000	20,800	184.14
Aug 2, 1978	470,000	70,000	203.28
Sept 6, 1978	470,000	133,600	212.50
Oct 3, 1978	470,000	134,400	223.68
Nov 1, 1978	470,000	80,000	224.02
Dec 6, 1978	470,000	20,000	196.06
Jan 3, 1979	470,000	16,400	219.34
Feb 7, 1979	470,000	59,200	252.53
Mar 7, 1979	470,000	—	241.68
Apr 4, 1979	470,000	—	239.51
May 2, 1979	470,000	—	246.18
June 6, 1979	444,000	—	280.39
July 4, 1979	444,000	—	281.52
Aug 1, 1979	444,000	—	289.59
Sept 5, 1979	444,000	—	333.24
Oct 3, 1979	444,000	—	412.78
Nov 7, 1979	444,000	—	393.55
Dec 5, 1979	444,000	—	426.37
Jan 2, 1980	444,000	—	562.85
Feb 6, 1980	444,000	—	712.12
Mar 5, 1980	444,000	—	641.23
April 2, 1980	444,000	—	481.01

Table 8.1 (contd)

US Treasury

		99.5% Pure		90% Pure	
Date		Ounces sold	Avg. price per ounce	Ounces sold	Avg. price per ounce
Jan 6, 1975		754,000	$153 to $185		
June 30, 1975		499,500	165.05		
May 23, 1978		300,000	180.38		
June 20, 1978		300,000	186.91		
July 18, 1978		300,000	185.16		
Aug 16, 1978		300,000	213.53		
Sept 19, 1978		300,000	212.76		
Oct 17, 1978		300,000	228.39		
Nov 21, 1978		750,000	199.05		
Dec 19, 1978		1,500,000	214.17		
Jan 16, 1979		1,000,000	219.71	500,100	$218.22
Feb 22, 1979		1,000,000	252.38	500,100	251.42
Mar 21, 1979		1,000,000	241.30	500,100	240.09
Apr 17, 1979		1,000,000	230.96	500,100	230.17
May 15, 1979				750,000	254.92
June 19, 1979				750,000	279.02
July 17, 1979				750,000	296.44
Aug 21, 1979				750,000	301.08
Sept 18, 1979				750,000	377.78
Oct 16, 1979				750,000	391.98
Nov 1, 1979				1,250,000	372.30

Source: American Institute for Economic Research

the International Monetary Fund and the Treasury Department of the United States of America.

Ironically, the people who have mismanaged the US gold stockpile chortle with glee at the 'profits' they have made by disposal of the 13 million or more ounces of gold for paper dollars that have declined in purchasing power. The reason for this 'profit' is that a base price of $43 an ounce is considered as a cost-reference for the gold in stock. What happened when the auctions halted? It added $200 an ounce to the value of gold.

Thus, to summarize the fundamental approach to gold price prediction, it is quite possible that supply/demand will play a very minor role in the price pattern but that two very important factors will play major roles: the size and frequency of the gold auctions and the rate of inflation, not only in America but also around the world. Gold is inextricably tied to the inflation rate: if that rate rises so will gold; if it falls, so will gold. Because of the influence of oil prices on the inflation rate, one can say that the price of gold is now tied to that of oil.

Technical research

The trader who is not interested in long-term trends but is out to try to profit every day, or at least once a week, may disregard the fundamental aspects of the gold picture and turn instead to the technical side of the research coin.

Jesse Livermore, king of commodity and stock speculators during the period 1906–1940, whose biography I once wrote, used to claim: 'If there's any easy money lying around Wall Street, no one's going to put it in your pocket.' But latter-day scalpers and traders evidently pay little heed to such wisdom and frenetically seek signals from charts to trigger their buy or sell decisions. I do not intend to provide the reader with a comprehensive course in technical trading or research. Instead, it makes sense to refer to the many books, treatises, essays and lectures available by devotees of bar charts, point-and-figure charts, cycle systems and so on.

What the technician tries to accomplish is simply to analyze whether or not gold is at any particular moment in trading time 'overbought' or 'oversold'. He also examines various 'momentum devices' which indicate that any movement up or down should or should not continue for some time in that direction. Moreover, there are areas of 'support' (which provide an underpinning for the price of gold in the market at certain levels) and 'resistance' (areas that could attract additional selling, preventing further price advance). In addition, bar charts may reflect volume and open interest and use various types of 'moving averages' along with the passage of time; while point and figure charts disregard the passage of time and volume and instead are purely interested in price reversals.

Of course, the fundamentalist is attempting through supply/demand to determine the major trend in the price of gold, while the technician seeks the minor trends to help the trader attack the market for profits either by trading from the short side (selling on strength and buying on weakness) or from the long side (buying on weakness and selling on strength). Whatever systems the technicians use, they are all absolutely infallible in analysing the past. But how accurate are they about predicting the future?

The question, of course, answers itself. Suffice to say that traders have to experiment and find their own technical 'thing'. We would avoid like the proverbial plague subscribing to any chart systems or technical trading methods that flamboyantly advertise how much money users have made in the past or how effective their charting systems have been. Experience has indicated that certain chart publishers, such as Commodity Research Bureau in America and Investment Research in Cambridge, England, produce the best bar charts suitable for most traders on gold and the other commodities. In the realm of point-and-figure, Conti Technical Services in Memphis, Tennessee produce the best charts.

Statistical (computerized) research

As to the computerized linear multiple regression approach, I can only say that such activity is often beyond both the pocket and the ken of the average reader who wants to make some money by trading gold metal or futures. Still, this approach has merit because it involves a rather simple concept. The unknown variable the trader seeks, of course, is the price, and that is on the left side of the equation. The unknown price in theory is formed from changes in the known factors. These known variables can consist of such diverse items as a parameter for the London fix, the current prime rate and the US inflation rate. In theory regressions involve the scattering of random prices which more or less form themselves near a certain central line. And if this trend continues, future prices should fall somewhere along or near this line. Irrespective of the ridicule that is often heaped upon this 'econometric' approach to price prediction, it does have some value as a check on the fundamentalist or the technician's approach to price prediction and is to be found in use at most large commodity brokerage firms.

Is it worth the expense and trouble for a trader to involve himself or herself in computer price models for gold? Well, Mocatta Metals has spent millions of dollars attempting to answer this question and is still not sure the effort was worth the expense. After all, in the final analysis prices on futures exchanges and physicals markets are made by people, not computers.

Other research sources for the private trader

What genuine advice can be given to a serious trader? If you are interested in trading in gold futures, your research should include daily inspection of the activity sheets of the various gold exchanges. It should also involve perusal of such daily newspapers as the *Financial Times, Journal of Commerce, New York Times, Wall Street Journal* and *American Metal Market*. In addition, various brokerage firms and bullion firms issue monthly, quarterly and/or annual reviews of the gold scene. Since the lion's share of free world gold production comes from South Africa, subscriptions to various periodicals from that country may also be worth while.

It is an old cliché that 'any philosophy that can be put in a nutshell belongs there'. We cannot compact gold research and trading philosophy into any nutshell, and so I must end this chapter by admitting that research theory is perhaps better than my explanation of it!

9

Gold funds and gold shares

For those who do not desire to undertake the obvious risks involved in placing funds in gold bullion or deposits on gold futures contracts, there are investment media which depend in many ways upon the price of gold but of course are not as 'good as gold'. By this I mean *gold shares* (shares in companies involved in mining the metal) and *gold funds* (closed-end or open-ended mutual funds and trusts which have the bulk of their assets invested in gold shares).

Since there are obvious extra charges and risks involved in trusting one's funds into the management of someone else I respectfully suggest that if possible investment in shares of any funds specializing in gold or gold investments be avoided. I will dispose of the 'funds' part of this chapter merely by cautioning the reader to investigate thoroughly the antecedents of the gold fund being offered by the persuasive salesmen before sending money. This is not to imply at all that investment in properly managed funds which specialize in gold shares will not bring either dividends or profits. Instead my attitude is simply a practical approach for a trader who may desire at times to go in and out of the share markets for small profits or losses. Obviously, fund managements are not free and some funds may charge fees for either acquisition or disposal, or both, which would preclude the trader from making commitments. So at the risk of sounding like an old iconoclast I would not purchase any gold share funds from the standpoint of future trading. If you are too busy to watch the shares markets and do not intend to trade for profits on occasion then perhaps gold share funds may be for you, but otherwise avoid them.

Table 9.1 South African gold mining share dividends

	Share price at 24 Apr 79 ($ per share)	Last four semi-annual gross dividends (declaration month) ($ per share)				Percentage yield, last 12 months divd. %
AMGOLD	25.88	.92(9)	.98(3)	1.15(9)	1.77(3)	11.3
Blyvoor	4.70	.29(6)	.34(12)	.38(6)	.46(12)	17.9
Buffels	12.38	1.03(6)	.69(12)	1.26(6)	.92(12)	17.6
Doorns	4.35	.11(6)	.23(12)	.34(6)	.23(12)	13.1
Durban Deep	5.90	–	–	–	.57(12)	9.7
East Drie	10.30	.40(6)	.49(12)	.46(6)	.86(12)	12.8
East Dagga	.28	–	.23(1)	.29(7)	–	103.6
ERGO	3.90	–	–	–	.29(4)	7.4
E.R.P.M.	4.13	–	–	–	.11(12)	2.7
Elsburg	1.36	.06(6)	.05(12)	.06(6)	.09(12)	11.0
Free State Ged.	23.25	1.72(10)	1.49(4)	2.13(10)	2.18(4)	18.5
Groots	1.86	.11(6)	.16(12)	.18(6)	.25(12)	23.1
Harmony	4.80	.29(9)	.34(3)	.43(9)	.62(3)	21.9
Harties	20.88	.80(6)	.86(12)	2.01(6)	1.26(12)	15.7
Kinrose	4.55	.25(9)	.26(3)	.37(9)	.37(3)	16.3
Kloof	9.50	.17(6)	.17(12)	.29(6)	.34(12)	6.6
Leslie	.94	.03(9)	.08(3)	.16(9)	.16(3)	34.0
Libanon	8.20	.46(6)	.46(12)	.69(6)	.58(12)	15.5
Loraine	1.12	–	–	–	–	–
Pres. Brand	14.63	.69(10)	.75(4)	.98(10)	1.36(4)	16.0
Pres. Steyn	11.25	.11(10)	.35(4)	.57(10)	.77(4)	11.9
Randfontein	43.25	1.72(6)	2.30(12)	2.30(6)	2.87(12)	12.0
St. Helena	12.25	.63(9)	.92(3)	1.26(9)	1.46(3)	22.2
Southvaal	8.10	–	.24(1)	–	.66(1)	8.1
Stilfontein	5.55	.13(6)	.13(12)	.18(6)	.58(12)	13.7
Vaal Reefs	23.25	.63(7)	.69(1)	1.15(7)	2.07(1)	13.8
Venterspost	3.30	.06(6)	.06(12)	.23(6)	.17(12)	12.1
Welkom	4.90	.32(10)	.29(4)	.46(10)	.50(4)	19.6
West Drie	31.88	1.67(6)	1.55(12)	2.87(6)	2.30(12)	16.2
Western Areas	2.10	.07(6)	.08(12)	.09(6)	.14(12)	11.0
Western Deep	11.25	.40(7)	.55(1)	.75(7)	.95(1)	15.1
Western Holdings	30.38	1.61(10)	2.18(4)	2.59(10)	3.19(4)	19.0
Winkelhaak	9.10	.54(9)	.61(3)	.87(9)	.94(3)	19.9

Source: Henry Brown

Gold shares, themselves, on the other hand, are quite desirable for the investor who may not want to take the trading risks offered by bullion or futures. There are good, sound companies based in America, Canada, Africa and other places practically all over the world which have a stake in the rise and fall of the price of gold bullion in the marketplace. Some companies, of course, are also involved rather heavily in other metals besides gold, and, in the case of the South African gold companies, uranium and its fortunes looms increasingly in importance as the price of oil soars.

Another aspect of risking funds in gold shares concerns the high dividends generally paid. In this regard, dividends of 15% and higher per year are not unusual. Henry Brown, who makes a regular study of the dividend action in South African gold mining shares, has kindly consented to permit me to list representative gold shares and their recent dividend history (Table 9.1).

The best single research source for keeping track of South African and other gold shares is *Mining Journal,* published by The Mining Journal Ltd, 15 Wilson Street, London EC2M 2TR, England. It issues a quarterly review of South African gold shares, and extracts from the August 1979 edition are reproduced here as Figs 9.1–9.4, by kind permission of The Mining Journal Ltd, to illustrate the layout and type of information given.

Fig. 9.1 illustrates the list of earnings statements of the major South African mining companies. Having delineated the operating results of these exciting ventures the review proceeds to list the price movements of the shares during the previous year (Fig. 9.2). Thereafter the listed mines are categorized as shown in Fig. 9.3: it should be realized that those mining companies listed as 'Developing Ventures' are very volatile and speculative, but may offer risk-takers the greatest chance for future long-term profits if the developing companies 'strike it rich'. Those companies with a listed life of 'about 10 Years or Less' also offer great risk, although generally paying a high dividend return. Marievale in Fig. 9.3, for example, represents 'break-up' or liquidation opportunity and the 46.2% dividend is in reality a liquidating payment. Companies listed as having a life of 'Over 20 Years' normally offer lower dividend yields than those with a lesser life; companies listed as 'Life 11–20 Years' generally offer higher dividends than those with longer lives.

Those mining companies listed under the rubric 'State Assisted' may have genuine merit in some cases and in others may be rank

REVENUE, COSTS AND EARNINGS SUMMARY
(in U.S. dollars)

MINE	JUNE QTR. '79 (R1 = $1·18)			MAR. QTR. '79 (R1 = $1·18)			DEC. QTR. '78 (R1 = $1·15)			SEPT. QTR. '78 (R1 = $1·15)		
	Rev./oz.	Costs/oz.	Earnings/share	Rev./oz.	Costs/oz.	Earnings/share	Rev./oz.	Costs/oz.	Earnings/share	Rev./oz.*	Costs/oz.	Earnings/share
Blyvooruitzicht	261·07	124·82	0·37	245·21	122·80	0·42	218·81	110·49	0·24	205·29	108·58	0·25
Bracken	264·38	114·47	0·14	244·00	105·81	0·13	215·50	103·04	0·11	210·42	98·84	0·13
Buffelsfontein	256·00	158·80	0·97	239·00	154·90	0·63	218·00	145·01	0·62	204·64	139·60	0·48
Doornfontein	255·87	147·72	0·32	241·74	146·53	0·32	219·17	136·62	0·33	201·20	131·37	0·24
Durban Deep	259·93	242·16	0·47	243·14	231·32	0·47	215·88	194·69	0·67	209·52	181·81	0·66
E. Driefontein	253·16	54·44	0·46	241·93	50·69	0·47	217·64	49·69	0·32	200·93	51·13	0·32
E. Rand Prop.	258·73	267·98	L0·19	238·90	252·78	0·19	217·85	238·88	0·07	204·25	234·96	0·02
Elandsrand	262·00	246·05	L0·27	245·00	493·16	L0·26	—	—	L0·41			
F. S. Geduld	259·00	94·04	1·29	238·00	97·93	1·10	219·00	89·18	1·08	197·00	76·82	0·93
F. S. Saaiplaas	259·00	256·11	L0·08	238·00	253·95	L0·07	214·00	234·01	L0·21	196·00	245·88	L0·03
Grootvlei	263·48	140·16	0·24	244·00	144·24	0·19	218·81	132·76	0·15	200·88	136·07	0·11
Harmony	258·47	n.a.	0·32	244·90	n.a.	0·47	219·87	n.a.	0·13	202·76	n.a.	0·26
Hartebeestfontein	268·43	122·21	1·84	247·13	129·01	0·99	213·92	119·07	0·91	206·34	115·46	0·78
Kinross	265·84	122·98	0·22	238·80	113·51	0·20	212·47	102·19	0·17	207·33	96·09	0·20
Kloof	253·96	81·61	0·48	237·82	84·36	0·39	217·31	82·91	0·31	201·95	82·22	0·26
Leslie	261·26	168·47	0·08	243·51	157·40	0·07	215·28	151·36	0·06	206·90	146·88	0·07
Libanon	256·94	139·19	0·54	238·77	129·58	0·50	217·66	123·03	0·44	203·12	120·09	0·37
Loraine	265·64	310·49	L0·01	248·51	289·40	0·01	218·96	256·61	—	219·07	215·14	0·07
Marievale	260·94	133·64	0·19	244·53	141·38	0·15	235·36	106·04	0·29	186·71	101·80	0·15
President Brand	258·00	112·97	0·39	239·00	105·57	0·55	216·00	102·38	0·54	192·00	104·39	0·32
President Steyn	258·00	135·91	0·60	239·00	138·98	0·55	216·00	147·26	0·30	200·00	130·50	0·25
Randfontein	256·62	163·32	3·20	238·20	130·66	3·55	219·65	98·08	3·36	203·37	75·89	0·59
St. Helena	254·44	98·61	0·81	217·54	93·91	0·83	215·66	88·83	0·64	207·57	84·37	0·51

Fig. 9.1 Operating results of South African gold mining companies, from *Mining Journal* quarterly review, August 1979.

PRICE MOVEMENTS 1979

	L'dn offshore ex-premium ($)			L'dn cum premium (£)			Johannesburg (R)			Dividends (R)		Grade Ratio %
	Jan. 9, '79	Apr. 10, '79	July 3, '79	Jan. 9, '79	Apr. 10, '79	July 3, '79	Jan. 9, '79	Apr. 10, '79	July 3, '79	1977-78	1978-79	
1. MAJOR FINANCE AND INVESTMENT COMPANIES												
Anglo American	4.28	5.92	6.79	3.02	3.44	3.30	6.75	7.45	7.85	0.37	0.46	—
Anglo American Gold Inv.	21.95	26.23	34.98	15.50	15.25	17.00	34.00	33.80	40.00	1.65	2.50	—
Anglo Transvaal 'A'	11.33	17.63	20.58	8.00	10.25	10.00	17.50	22.75	23.50	1.15	1.50	—
Barlow Rand	3.19	4.34	4.94	2.25	2.52	2.40	4.93	5.65	5.55	0.28	0.33	—
Charter Cons.	1.91	2.86	3.00	1.35	1.66	1.46	4.00	4.30	3.10	0.246	0.246	—
Cons. Gold Fields	2.59	3.89	4.46	1.83	2.26	2.17	5.70	6.10	5.30	0.246	0.276	—
De Beers	5.74	6.45	7.45	4.05	3.75	3.62	8.80	8.25	8.37	0.53	0.65	—
General Mining	5.10	7.23	9.26	3.60	4.20	4.50	7.85	9.20	10.50	0.45	0.60	—
Gold Fields of S.A.	17.35	26.23	34.98	12.25	15.25	17.00	27.00	33.50	39.75	1.10	1.55	—
J.C.I.	19.83	26.66	32.41	14.00	15.50	15.75	31.00	33.50	36.30	1.70	1.80	—
Lydenburg Plats	1.03	1.50	1.58	0.73	0.87	0.77	1.65	1.80	1.80	0.01	0.12	—
Middle Wits.	2.38	4.30	4.73	1.68	2.50	2.30	3.80	5.50	5.10	0.25	0.35	—
Rustenburg Plat	1.49	2.34	2.39	1.05	1.36	1.16	2.33	2.90	2.68	—	0.13	—
Sentrust	2.45	3.17	4.18	1.73	1.84	2.03	3.85	4.15	4.70	0.30	0.38	—
T.C. Land	18.41	30.11	29.32	13.00	17.50	14.25	29.50	38.80	32.75	1.00	1.17	—
U.C. Investments	3.12	4.20	5.04	2.20	2.44	2.45	4.85	5.25	6.20	0.34	0.45	—
Union Corporation	3.82	5.57	6.89	2.70	3.24	3.35	6.05	7.05	8.00	0.38	0.47	—
2. GOLD MINING COMPANIES												
Afrikander Lease	2.53	3.96	4.24	1.73	2.30	2.06	3.80	5.05	4.75	—	—	—
Blyvoor	3.89	4.77	6.38	2.75	2.77	3.10	6.00	6.00	7.20	0.63	1.05	50
Bracken	1.03	1.24	1.65	0.73	0.72	0.80	1.60	1.60	1.85	0.32	0.48	55
Buffels	11.02	13.16	14.69	7.78	7.65	7.14	17.15	17.00	16.70	1.70	2.00	35
Deelkraal	1.27	2.08	3.07	0.90	1.21	1.49	2.02	2.65	3.50	—	—	—
Doornfontein	3.20	4.56	5.82	2.26	2.65	2.83	4.85	5.80	6.60	0.50	0.60	39
East Driefontein	9.28	10.77	13.44	6.55	6.26	6.53	14.50	13.75	15.10	0.83	1.30	78

Fig. 9.2 Price movements of South African gold mining companies' shares, from *Mining Journal* quarterly review, August 1979

CLASSIFICATION OF MINES

Category		Working Costs R/kg	$/oz	Share Price (New York) $	Dividend US cents	Gross Yield %
1. Developing Ventures						
Afrikander Lease	U	—	—	4.24	—	—
Elandsrand		6704	246.04	6.83	—	—
Deelkraal		—	—	3.07	—	—
†FS Saaiplaas	U	6978	256.09	1.83	—	—
Unisel		—	—	5.02	—	—
2. Life Over 20 Years (Better quality gold mines)						
East Driefontein		1483	54.44	13.44	153	11.4
Kloof		2224	81.61	12.82	130	10.1
Southvaal	U	3068	112.60	10.80	67	6.2
Western Deeps	u	2450	89.91	15.45	209	13.5
3. Life 11–20 Years (Better quality gold mines)						
Buffels	U	4327	158.79	14.69	236	16.1
Doornfontein		4025	147.71	5.82	71	12.1
Ergo	U			4.73	29	6.1
†FS Geduld	u U	2562	94.03	27.00	437	16.2
Harmony	U	5081‡	186.48‡	7.39	106	14.3
Hartes		3330	122.21	28.82	472	16.4
Kinross		3351	122.97	6.28	76	12.1
Libanon		3793	139.19	11.81	177	15.0
†P. Brand		3078	112.96	18.21	236	13.0
†P. Steyn	u	3703	135.90	15.21	136	8.9
Randfontein	U	4450	163.31	49.38	590	11.9
St. Helena		2687	98.61	17.08	277	16.2
Vaal Reefs	U	3783	138.84	32.92	437	13.3
Western Areas		4955	181.86	2.76	28	10.1
Winkelhaak		2300	84.41	13.44	184	13.7
4. Life about 10 Years or Less						
Blyvoor	U	3401	124.82	6.38	124	19.4
Bracken		3119	114.47	1.65	57	34.5
Grootvlei		3819	140.15	2.72	68	25.0
Marievale		3641	133.63	1.67	92	55.1
†Welkom	u	4630	169.92	5.68	97	17.1
West Driefontein		1628	59.76	44.49	726	16.3
†W. Holdings	u	2397	87.97	32.92	584	17.7
5. State Assisted						
Durban Deep		6597	242.10	8.54	106	12.4
ERPM		7301	267.94	9.05	24	2.7
Leslie		4590	168.46	1.44	33	22.9
Loraine		8461	310.52	1.65	—	—
*Stilfontein	U	4641	170.33	6.44	100	15.5
Venterspost		7072	259.56	4.42	53	12.0
WR Consolidated	U	16543	607.11	2.92	21	7.2
Wit Nigel		6498	238.48	0.93	2	2.0

Notes

U — Uranium of major importance.

u — Uranium of minor importance.

† — Members of the JMS. Treatment of slimes will probably continue after mining operations cease.

‡ — After allowing costs of R3 ($3.5)/ton for uranium treatment. This will allow treatment to continue after mining operations have ceased.

* — Has large volumes of slimes with good uranium grades. This will allow treatment to continue after mining operations have ceased.

(a) — In the case of mines with a significant uranium contribution the working costs are overstated if one allows for uranium profits.

(b) — Life classification has been based on reasonable assumptions as to the trend of the gold price and working costs. It indicates the life of the operation at approximately full capacity. No allowance has been made for a lower rate of production in later years or for the possible treatment of surface dump material.

Fig. 9.3 Classification of South African gold mines, from *Mining*

speculation on rapid and sustained gold price increase. According to *Mining Journal,* 'When the gold price is rising at an above average rate, certain of these shares may be expected to outperform the market despite the reservations regarding their basic possibilities.'

So which of the list would have such merit? That question is intriguing, and rewarding when the risk-taker comes up with the right answer. At the time of writing, of all the companies in the state assisted category, one that holds obvious promise is Stilfontein—and oddly enough its promise stems more from uranium than from gold. Fig. 9.4 presents a short extract from *Mining Journal* quarterly review's analysis of Stilfontein (each individual mine is given this treatment). From the commentary printed under the tabular information in the review, it is clear that this is one mining stock which should not be sold short.

Gold mining shares are not, of course, restricted to South Africa. A goodly selection of both promotional and operating gold mine shares has been sold to the public since the first gold rush to California in 1848. As a result, investors can today find gold stocks on the New York Stock Exchange, the American Stock Exchange, the American over-the-counter market, and on just about every other stock exchange on earth.

In America, for example, the New York Stock Exchange lists for trading Campbell Red Lake and Dome Mines (Canadian producers) and Homestake (America's largest producing gold mine). The American Stock Exchange lists for trading Giant Yellowknife and Wright Hargreaves. All South African shares in America are bought and sold through brokerage firms that deal in over-the-counter as well as in listed shares and the Toronto and Montreal Stock Exchanges, as well as Vancouver, list a myriad of speculative non-producing gold mining companies that could someday go into action if the price of the metal advanced enough to make operating such mines a practical, money-making enterprise for the developers. Assuredly, readers who are interested in becoming either investors or traders in gold shares will find a plethora of literature and advice freely given by brokerage firms all over the earth. There are certain advisers such as Michael Levinson, Ira Cobleigh, James Dines, James Sinclair, Eliot Janeway and a whole host of others, for years labeled 'goldbugs', who fervently believe in the future of properly selected and monitored gold mining share portfolios.

STILFONTEIN

Group: General Mining	Location: Klerksdorp	Produces: Gold only

Full name: Stilfontein Gold Mining Co. Ltd.
Issued capital: R6,531,460 (13,062,920 shares of R0·5 each)
Loan capital: R838,000   Net current assets: R5,999,000

Gold price received:

	1975	1976	1977	1978	1979
$/oz	131	120	146	197	248
R/kg	3,653	3,355	4,079	5,520	6,833

Dividends usually paid: August and February
Loan levies recoverable: R720,000
ADR: Morgan G., Citibank, Irving T., Chem.B.
Share price range: '77: 220c to 410c   118p to 296p
                   '78: 340c to 725c   206p to 331p
                   '79: 640c to 820c   291p to 450p
Financial year ends: December 31   Date of last a/c: March 30. 1979

Extent of claim area: 3.105 hectares   Lease formula: $y = 23 - \dfrac{138}{X}$
Other land holdings and/or options: Mineral rights over a total area of
                                      742 hectares. 2.051 hectares
                                      freehold
Share holdings: 85% of Chemwes Ltd.

	Year	Basis $/oz R/kg	Tons (000)	Gold g R/kg	Equiv. cm-g	Uran. kg	Equiv. cm-kg
	1974	189·5 4191	4.106	11·9 1.432	—	—	
	1975	133·4 3730	4,155	12·7 1.519	—	—	
	1976		3,187	13·6 1.630	—	—	
Ore	1977	155·0 4333	3,222	13·5 1.620	0·17	20·37
Reserves:	1979†	280·0 7601	1,970	12·8 1.538	0·18	21·73

Milling began: 1952   Present monthly mill capacity: 181,000 tons
Sorting rate: 1975, 35·6%; 1976, 39·7%; 1977, 40·1%; 1978, 38·4%

MILLING RESULTS

	DEVELOPMENT			MILLING RESULTS								
	Metres sampled	Payability		Tons Milled	Grade rec.	Costs				Working Profit	Revenue from Gold	
Period		%	Ave. cm g		g per ton	Per ton		Per oz		Per ton		
	(000)			(000)		Rand		$		Rand	(R000)	
31·12·74	4·8	71	1824	1932	8·2	18.36		102.65		9.76	54324	
31·12·75	5·6	67	1676	1768	8·3	25.56		110.42		4·68	53200	
31·12·76	4·4	64	1783	1893	8·7	27.89		114.93		1·22	55108	
31·12·77	3·6	58	1916	1904	8·6	34.80		144.51		0·34	66906	
31·12·78	4·4	63	2225	1958	8·5	37.90		160.09		8·85	91530	
Mar. Qtr.	1·0	71	2322	474	8·3	37.75		162.72		3·22	19419	
June Qtr.	1·1	56	2425	504	8·3	35.59		153.48		8·96	22451	
Sept. Qtr.	1·3	68	2190	486	8·8	38.51		160.16		10·32	23731	
Dec. Qtr.	1·3	59	2005	494	8·7	39.81		164.04		12·68	25929	
Mar. Qtr.	1·2	75	2269	463	8·5	39.16		168.71		17·47	26368	
June Qtr.	2·0	72	2058	515	8·1	37.41		170.34		19·18	29142	
30-6-78	2·1	63	2370	978	8·3	36.64		157·96		6·17	41870	
30-6-79	3·2	73	2141*	978	8·3	38·34		169·55		18·52	55510	

FINANCIAL RESULTS

	Working Profit (R000)	Net* Sundry Revenue (R000)	Tax and/or Lease (R000)	Net Profit after T/L (R000)	Capital Expendi-ture (R000)	Earnings/ share after T/L and C. Ex. Cents	Divs. Paid Cents
	17929	2187	8987	11129	3800	56	65·0
	8609(g)	1981	212	10378	6135	32	36·0
	5245(g)	1181	610	5816	1985	29	22·0
	6122(g)	423	7	6308	3597	23	22·0
	17306(g)	3723	6206	14823	3128	90	66·0
	1778(g)	131	58	1851	709	9	
	4247(g)	450	609	4088	800	25	16·0
	5017	2790	3399	4408	466	30	
	6264	372	2623	4013	1149	22	50·0
	8235	1051	5910	4276	231	31	
	9876	Dr.964	4780	4132	481	28	35·0
	6025(g)	581	667	5939	1509	34	16·0
	18111	87	9790	8408	712	59	35·0

Year to: 1978   1979   6 mths. to

*Includes net State assistance   (g) Includes acid profit   *Includes acid profit   † As at June 30. 1979

COMMENT

Uranium Will Help

Mining began at Stilfontein in 1952 and in March 1979 the chairman estimated that underground operations would continue for a further five years although a new project to recover uranium from surface slimes dams would have a longer future. The mine has had difficulty in maintaining mill tonnage from its own lease area in recent years because insufficient stope face has been available. In the latest quarter, however, the mill tonnage improved, and production was further boosted by the processing of sludge from the waste washing plant and surface dump.

In an effort to make available more working face, development on the Vaal Reef was increased in 1978 to 30,635m. Of this, 7,554m were in an area in the south-east portion of the lease where the Vaal Reef was unexpectedly found to the east of the Kromdraai fault. Values here have been high but the area has proved to be heavily faulted requiring excessive development.

Consequently, even the large amount of development completed in 1978 was insufficient to replace ore reserves depleted during the year.

At the end of 1978 ore reserves calculated at $205/oz totalled 2·78 million tons at 13·1 g/ton. Owing to an error in uranium values, up-dated and corrected figures have now been published for reserves at June 30, 1979. Based on $280/oz, ore reserves increased to 3·73 million tons at 12·1 g/ton, of which 44% will require additional development to make it available for mining. The rate of development has increased again in the past two quarters, with good results in terms of uranium values and the tonnage available for mining.

New Project

Stilfontein has decided to embark on a project to recover uranium oxide from surface slimes and a separate company, Chemwes Ltd., has been set up for this purpose. This move may be partly for administrative convenience and also in the hope of some tax concession. A plant to treat 270,000 ton/month of slimes has been completed ahead of schedule and is now being commissioned. A long-term sales contract for a substantial part of the annual production at competitive prices has been finalised, starting in the second half of 1980. The capital cost of the project will be R77·25 million; a long-term loan of R50 million has been arranged and a further loan and overdraft facilities will be used to complete the financing. Apart from this, capital expenditure in 1979 is expected to total R3·22 million.

The marginal nature of Stilfontein's operations is illustrated by the consistent narrowing of profit margins between 1974 and 1977. The mine was in receipt of State assistance from 1975 to 1977. However, in 1978 the gold price improved by more than one third to $197/oz and profitability recovered to such an extent that a threefold increase of dividend to 66c per share was well covered. A further rise in the gold price in 1979 has improved distributable earnings to 59c per share and the interim to 35c per share.

Good development values in the Kromdraai area and the planned resumption of uranium production have revived interest in Stilfontein despite the fact that the potential life of the mine is at the lower end of the SHORT category.

MINING JOURNAL—Quarterly Review of South African Gold Shares

Fig. 9.4 Information on an individual South African gold mine (Stilfontein), from *Mining Journal* quarterly review, August 1979

59

Using '20/20 hindsight' it becomes immediately obvious that these gentlemen really had something some years ago. How well their investment theories will work in the future will be borne out by what happens to the price of gold in the marketplace and the concomitant costs of digging it out of the ground. In early 1978 the cost of creating an ounce of gold in South Africa was about $135 and by the end of 1979 that cost had approached $300. As labor demands more for its efforts and as that country gravitates toward political and economic change, anything might happen to the costs of mining gold and preparing it in bar form for the marketplace.

That is why from my viewpoint I would rather remain actively trading in the gold futures markets, or combining trading in bullion with futures, than dabbling in shares of mining companies where anything could happen, not only to the management, but also to the country in which the management operates.

But having dutifully mentioned some of the areas for both risk-takers and investors it is time to return to the world of price change as it occurs daily in the arenas of the gold futures markets and the international currency markets.

10

Gold systems and planning

Trading gold with currencies

Although the price of gold is universally quoted in dollars, citizens of countries other than the United States do, of course, govern their existence around currencies other than dollars. Until the end of 1978, the price of gold depended heavily on the strength or weakness of the dollar. Since gold prices are quoted in dollars it is quite understandable that if the Swiss Franc rose in value against the dollar, the price of gold for the Swiss declined. In like manner the Germans and Japanese found times during 1978 when the price of gold rose in actual dollars but their currencies at the same time also rose much more against the dollar, with the result that even though the dollar price of gold had risen, gold indeed became less expensive for the Germans and Japanese who held their own currencies. Fig. 10.1 shows the relative price of gold in US dollars, Swiss Francs and German Marks for the period February 1978 to January 1979. Thus, if a Swiss citizen had to sell Swiss Francs to buy gold, he could have hedged simultaneously by buying futures contracts in the Swiss Franc on the Chicago IMM; and as his currency rose in value against the dollar and gold rose in dollar price value the Swiss trader did not lose the value of his currency that had been locked into gold bullion or futures. Americans too could have resorted to such strategies—and in fact many sophisticated traders did go long in the 'strong' currencies (the German Mark, the Japanese Yen and the Swiss Franc) while they acquired a hedge in gold against inflation.

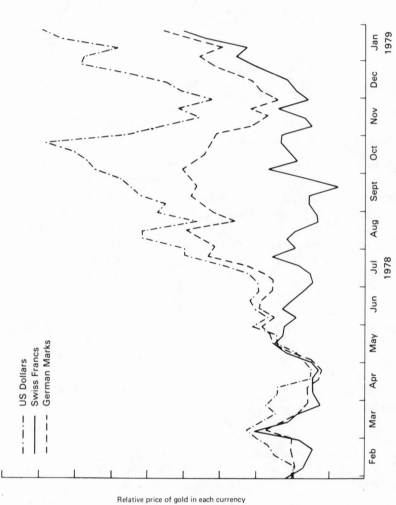

Fig. 10.1 Relative movement of price of gold in three currencies, February 1978–January 1979 (data copyright of Mocatta Metals Corporation)

Another trading system involved a sort of arbitrage between currencies and gold futures or bullion. In this instance, the trader went long in the strong currencies and simultaneously went short in gold bullion or futures.

But how often we have to unlearn what we have learnt from markets in order to relearn what should be done when conditions change. When President Carter summoned massive monetary means for broad intervention in foreign exchange markets in order to 'rescue' the dollar, the dollar of course underwent a period of stability that made trading in gold and currencies at the same time a rather pointless exercise. Another result was that the OPEC nations realized that although they were sitting on the major portion of about $600 billion dollars, the US Government had done nothing at all to stem the rising rate of inflation inside the country and therefore the dollars already on hand at OPEC plus the dollars they were going to get for their oil sales would decrease rapidly in purchasing power. Therefore oil price rises were accelerated, causing greater inflation in the United States and in the process round the world.

This changed the golden ball game for the trader and caused the wise ones to abandon the gold/currency ploys and instead turn to the relationship of gold against the price of a barrel of oil. Since the heating oil futures traded on the New York Mercantile Exchange are too thin, at the time of writing, for venturesome traders to position, the traders went back to playing the gold/silver ratio.

Trading gold against silver

According to Chauncey Depew (President of the New York Central Railroad, US Senator and the most popular after-dinner speaker in America near the turn of the century), 'When Columbus discovered America, ten ounces of silver were equal to one of gold . . . When the Pilgrim Fathers landed on Plymouth Rock, thirteen ounces of silver were equal to one of gold.' Then in a speech against William Jennings Bryan in 1896 he thundered: 'When you say sixteen ounces of silver are equal to one of gold, you are perpetrating a monstrous fraud, because we know enough of the conditions in the world today to know it takes thirty-two ounces of silver to buy one ounce of gold.'

Fig. 10.2 is a chart for the gold/silver ratio covering the year from April, 1979, to April, 1980. Notice that at the end of April

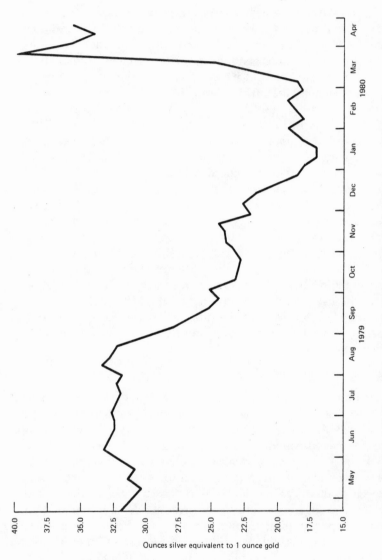

Fig. 10.2 Gold/silver ratio, April 1979–April 1980 (data copyright of Mocatta Metals Corporation)

through July, 1979, the relationship between silver and gold was just about the same as it was 84 years ago!

How does a trader today employ the gold/silver ratio systematically for trading profits? A glance at Fig. 10.2 indicates that the ratio has ranged during the year April 1979–April 1980 from a high of close to above 40:1 to a low of about 17:1. What does this mean? It is simply a measure of volatility on the part of the two precious metals, so that a trader, when the ratio approaches 40:1, reasons that gold has gone up too fast and should be sold short while silver has not gone up fast enough and should be bought long. Actually, to the ratio trader it doesn't matter if the actual prices of gold and silver rise together or fall together. If the prices fall and the ratio widens, then silver has dropped too fast and too much against declining gold and a trading correction should ensue. Conversely, if the ratio narrows down to, say, 20:1, then in a rising market silver has leaped far faster than gold and should have a correction. In that case, the gold would be positioned on the long side and silver shorted simultaneously. If the ratio narrows in a falling market, then the ratio trader reasons that gold has gone down too fast and too much in relation to silver and should be bought while silver should be sold, and so on.

In the last quarter of 1978, for instance, I noticed opportunities to make plenty of money trading the ratio; and during December 1978 and January 1979 I became convinced that the gold/silver ratio during 1979 would continue to narrow as silver made up the lag behind gold that occurred in 1978. During 1979, silver advanced much more rapidly than gold and the ratio plummeted below 20:1 by year end. Then in the ensuing price collapse of silver that began on January 21, 1980, the trend in the ratio reversed and during March it approached 45:1! Traditionally this indicates that gold is out of line and is overpriced in relation to past silver values, etc.

Dollar averaging

In addition to trading the gold/silver ratio, going long and short in the appropriate futures at the proper times, traders use other systems involving formula timing and dollar averaging.

In this regard the trader decides to attack the futures market either from the long side or the short side at preset price levels. If, for example, the trader guesses that the price of September gold on the Comex will range for the next few months between $500

and $600 an ounce he will buy at preset points, e.g., one con-
tract at every $5 below $565, and on strength would sell one
contract every $5 an ounce increase over $570. Of course, the $5
per ounce change is simply an arbitrary number and can be
altered to suit the trader's wants—or I should say, intestinal
fortitude! It follows that if the trader decided to trade September
gold from the short side he would reverse the above system by
selling first at every $5 interval over $570 an ounce short and
covering every $5 an ounce below $565 by offsetting his shorts
with buys in the same contract months.

Dollar averaging, of course, can be applied to regularly
scheduled purchases of bullion whether the investor uses the
Citibank plan or Mocatta Delivery Orders. In using similar dollar
amounts to purchase gold bullion at regular intervals the investor
is getting more mileage than if he had used the same amount of
money in an 'arithmetical' averaging approach.

Monitoring share prices and interest rates

There are many relationships between the going price of gold and
other forms of investments. For example, it is pretty well ac-
knowledged that if gold moves up then common stocks on the
New York Stock Exchange should move down. In his provocative
and innovative thesis 'Can gold lose its glitter?' Eric Steen Seiersen illustrates how the price of gold has acted in comparison with
both the Dow-Jones Industrial Average and interest rates inside
the United States from 1972 through most of 1978 (Fig. 10.3).

While such relationships may not always persist, at least examination of both the condition of interest rates and the stock
market could signal a trader as to whether the basic trend of gold
prices is liable to be up or down for the foreseeable future. Of
course, should interest rates drop sharply in the United States it
would normally signal that inflation has been slowed and
perhaps the prices of precious metals might reverse their two-
year trend. But with oil bringing pressure on the upside of
inflation such a reversal is hardly probable at this time. In any
event, as Mr. Seiersen states, 'The price of gold will probably be a
good deal higher ten years from now. But in the course of this
upwards trend, the gold market will experience normal (interim)
bull and bear trends. And these trends should provide a mirror
image of the US stock market—with gold rising when stocks fall,
and vice versa.'

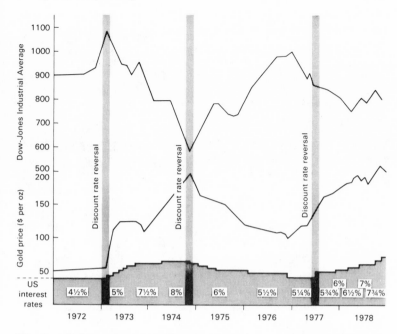

Fig. 10.3 Relationship of gold prices to Dow-Jones Industrial Average and US interest rates (source: E. S. Seiersen)

Trading the auction

Another approach to profits in a systematic manner which has been possible at least since May, 1978, and which can continue until the United States stops its gold auctions, is 'trading the auction'. Especially in 1979, every time a monthly auction approached, gold prices on the futures exchanges took an upward trend. This, of course, permitted bullion dealers and other interested traders to go short in advance of bidding for the bullion from the Treasury sale. Now one might think under normal circumstances that the advent of a new supply of the metal into the physical marketplace each month would not only depress the market but also pull down the futures markets. Strangely enough—and as if the public wanted to keep reminding its government that the auctions are wrong—the gold price also has always *appreciated* after the auction. So again, traders had their choice if they wanted to play against the auction in either the bullion or the futures markets.

In the bullion markets it has paid to position bullion a week or so in advance of the auction and then dispose of the bullion several days after the auction as the price worked higher. In the futures market longs could have been put into position before each auction, say a week or so, and on balance sold out a week or so after the auction at profits.

Physicals or futures?

The story goes that had an investor purchased 100 shares of IBM when it made its début in 1914 and had held the shares till today the investor, if still alive, would have an equity of several million dollars. In like vein, had an investor positioned several thousand ounces of gold at $43 an ounce in 1969, as Crédit-Suisse did, his portfolio today would have reflected rather handsome long-term gains. But how many traders who owned IBM at the beginning held on till today without disposing of the original shares? And how many traders bought bullion way back and never sold it? The answers are obvious. An investor may make long-term profits but may never live to enjoy them. At least a trader who goes in and out of exciting markets like gold, silver and platinum has some fun, to say the least.

As to price trends for gold, Robert Guy of N. M. Rothschild & Sons Limited, London, has pointed out that Walter Frey of the Swiss Bank and Fritz Plass of the Deutsche Bank 'decried an American tendency to be dominated by local technical considerations, were suspicious of the true motives of the Commission House [American futures commission merchant] and Floor Broker mentality [the scalpers] and above all felt that futures market operators were ill-informed of the fundamental factors affecting the market. As Mr. Frey put it, "Price trends in the United States all too often are based on factors whose relevance to the physical gold market is strictly limited." '

Whilst these eminent European gentlemen may have grave reservations about the tactics and practices of traders who go in and out the gold futures markets almost daily, the main point is that the mechanism and the opportunity exists for any sophisticated trader to study actions and tactics of futures trading and on balance profit from it—or contain losses to a limited sum of money. Whatever system a trader decides to put into use and whatever factors prompt his or her decision to attack the problem of profits from the long side, the short side or even both ways (I have seen traders long and short of the market in different gold months, who unwound both legs of their spread at different times and for profits each time!), what is most important is that an eminent gold trader like Mr. Guy concludes: 'I am certainly not against futures markets but the gold market cannot rely on them alone. Their functioning can only be enhanced not only by the participation of the traditional bullion dealer but also by the presence of a parallel market of sophisticated and well-informed physical specialists.'

To this I might add that one can become perhaps with a good deal of study and hard work a 'well-informed physical specialist' but it takes *capital*—millions and millions of dollars—to make it big in the physicals market. On the other hand, informed traders who operate with some sort of systematic approach to futures trading in gold can make a lot of money with much smaller capital. A serious futures trader, nevertheless, would need at least $100,000 to $250,000 of risk funds available to even dream of making a million dollars or more from the gold markets.

Evolving a trading plan

The risk taker should do the following before risking even one dollar, pound or franc:

1. Study intensely the price movements in gold futures in New York and Chicago of the recent past.
2. Study intensely the daily changes in the London gold market of the recent past.
3. Project what the inflation rate in the United States will be for the six months after the trader intends to speculate.
4. Project what the price of oil will be for the six months after the trading plan will go into action so that both cash markets and OPEC oil prices are considered trendwise.
5. Project what will happen to the economies of the so-called strong-currency countries (Japan, West Germany and Switzerland) for at least a year after the trading plan is destined to commence.
6. From conclusions drawn from the above economic study, make considered guesses on where the price of gold could go on both the upside and the downside in London and the futures markets for the next six months or year.
7. Having made your price estimates now it is time to consider the practical mechanics of operating the account. This includes

making decisions as to what point to enter the physicals or futures markets, or even options markets, and in what direction; how much capital is to be committed to a single trade; how much loss should be limited to; and what target price should trigger dissolution of the position.

While I cannot help you too much here on setting up self-education in the field of international economics, I can try to assist you with some yardsticks in setting up a trading plan.

Gold trading plan

1. Never commit more than half the amount of money you have decided to risk. Thus, if an account is designed to involve $50,000, do not commit at any one time more than $25,000 to the marketplace. Use the other $25,000 to earn interest on Government or money market instruments or bank accounts.
2. Limit any possible loss to 25% of the total account. Thus if setting up a plan to trade actively in gold futures involving a total of $50,000, close out the account if you lose $12,500. If you lose that much then your approach has been wrong; a wrong plan needs revision.
3. Do not hesitate to seek advice and counsel from experienced people who have a good reputation and a good track record at commodity firms which are members of leading exchanges. But, if you have the time and the patience, operate the trading plan you have devised all by yourself. You certainly wouldn't want to have someone else play a round of golf for you, but it might make sense to have an experienced caddy advise what club to use on a difficult approach shot.
4. Keep your gold trading plan flexible and don't hesitate to 'fine tune' it by making changes as needed. If you cannot unlearn errors your plan will fail.
5. 'Paper trade' for at least a month so as to learn without suffering financial loss. In so doing make market decisions, calculate margins, calculate daily equity and enter imaginary stop-loss orders ·on the sell side for imaginary longs and imaginary buy-stops for imaginary shorts.
6. While paper trading, become familiar with at least three top commodity brokerage firms. Read their daily wires and advisories and any fundamental and technical reports recently issued on gold or other precious metals.
7. Decide what kind of charts to follow and what kind of moving

averages or other technical devices you want in order to keep price movement action in front of you graphically. Remember: every chart, no matter how complicated or simple it may be, reflects only past action and interpretations of future price activity are the province of the person examining and interpreting the past as shown by the charts.

8. Read everything you can about gold, gold futures trading and market activity in the regular newspapers (*New York Times, Financial Times, Wall Street Journal, Journal of Commerce* etc.), and if you can afford the expense read *The American Metal Market* (a daily metal trades paper). Also, you might subscribe to *Gold and Silver Report* (Newtown, Connecticut) and any other gold advisory letters available. Subscription costs are in most cases tax-deductible. Certain gold conferences are held at several times a year in various places in the world by the National Committee for Monetary Reform (New Orleans, Louisiana), the American Metal Market (New York) and the *Financial Times* organization (London). A note to any of these organizations will bring you the meeting dates. Not only are these conferences tax-deductible and normally pleasurable educational opportunities but they also boast as speakers some of the world's leading people in the gold industry.

9. *Do-it-yourself:* Having followed all the previous suggestions and having successfully paper traded for at least a month in the various gold markets it is time to implement your trading plan and put it into action. Then when your plan gets going watch its progress and make suitable alterations. If possible, *do not give discretionary powers to anybody.* There's an old saying, 'discretion given is money lost'. And besides, there's no fun if you really want to trade and someone else is doing it for you. In this regard I am reminded of some cogent lines from John Godfrey Saxe, now long-forgotten but once America's most widely read and renowned poet:

> In battle or business, whatever the game,
> In law or in love, it is ever the same;
> In the struggle for power, or the scramble for pelf,
> Let this be your motto—*Rely on yourself!*

On this pontifical note it would be fitting, of course, to end this book. But I have not yet touched upon gold's future, which forms the subject of the next chapter.

11

The golden future

Back in 1893 the United States suffered from a severe panic occasioned in part by failure of the British banking house of Baring Brothers, which caused Continental investors to unload American securities, draining the US Treasury gold reserve to below the $100 million mark. Needless to say, American currency wasn't welcome abroad in paper form. But by 1904 the Treasury, through the floating of gold bonds and other devices, had managed to replenish the gold pool and America was well on the way back to the 'age of gold'. Reporting on the recovery, the Hon. Chauncey Depew claimed:

> The one act which has done more than all the others to assure the wage earner his full share in the fruits of his skill and the protection of his savings has been the gold dollar and the establishment of gold as a standard of value. The worker in every field knows that by this compensation, which he receives for what he gives, he has a purchasing power for the living of himself and family which is subject to no vicissitudes or disastrous fluctuations.

Sad to say, it is difficult for American Presidents to learn from history. When Mr. Carter abandoned the peanut business to attempt to manage an obviously unmanageable bureaucracy one of the strategies effected in 1978 in the wake of an obviously slipping dollar was a resumption of the Treasury gold sales. Several sales had occurred in 1975 to supply an adequate amount of gold for Americans, who had been prevented legally for more than forty-two years from owning bullion, and then wisely the sales had been stopped, after about 1.25 million ounces had been dumped at prices ranging from $153 to $185 an ounce.

But the resumption of gold sales on a monthly basis in 1978 and the subsequent acceleration of the amounts involved in each sale gave rise to the following questions:

1. If the sales had continued at the rate of 1.5 million ounces a month there would have been no gold in the Treasury in fifteen years: what would the US dollar have been worth then against the currencies of countries that had gold in their central banks?
2. Would the US Government continue by its intransigent attitude to divorce gold from its traditional monetary role while other countries, including developing Third-World nations, were strengthening their currencies via gold purchases?

The change in the amount of gold to be auctioned which was announced in spring 1979 by the United States Government, whereby the monthly quantity was halved from 1.5 million ounces to 750,000 ounces, and the purity of the gold involved in the auction changed from preponderantly 995 gold to totally 900 gold, has given rise to almost as much speculation in economics classrooms as it has in the gold pits of the futures markets in New York and Chicago.

Concurrently with the sudden change in attitude and the amount of gold to be auctioned, America's European trading partners initiated the European Monetary System, which was founded on a basis of a 20% contribution in gold by each government joining the system.

This all gives rise to conjecture about the future role of gold in the monetary system and where the price of gold will go if the metal indeed is returned to its rightful role as a reserve for the paper in circulation. Among the questions that the golden future will answer are:

1. Will the United States halt the gold auctions—permanently?
2. Will the United States, which prior to 1975 held more than 70% of the gold in the central banks of the free world, decide to replenish the gold (about 14 million ounces) already sold from the stockpile?
3. Will the Soviet Union be compelled to dump massive amounts of gold on the free world market in exchange for Western currencies to purchase needed grains, metals, etc.?
4. Will the current and succeeding American Administrations be able to contain or cope with the alarming inflation rate (currently running at admitted rates of 18%, but really surging at 25% at the time of writing)?

5. Will the inflation rates of the so-called 'strong-currency' countries rise alarmingly this year and next year because of their dependence on oil?

All of the above constitutes a sampling of the kind of questions whose answers will affect the price of gold in the marketplace. Obviously, the answers I might supply to any of these questions would be sheer and perhaps erroneous conjecture. But I can supply some projections as to what will happen to the price of gold depending on which way these debatable questions are answered.

To begin with the first question: in retrospect the United States has sold off about 14 million ounces of gold at prices about $180 less per ounce than the current gold fixing. This represents to my way of thinking a loss to American taxpayers of almost a billion dollars. In addition, assets that have been sold off have ap- preciated over $180 an ounce while the dollars received for their sale have been losing purchasing power significantly (I would say at the rate of 20% per year and not be making a wild guess). How long the electorate will stand for such mismanagement of publicly owned property is anyone's guess. But it is reasonable to surmise that, at future elections, if politics and policy do not work for the good of the electorate, the politicians will be changed. Thus, when by some miracle the gold auctions were halted in November, 1979, the price of gold rose another $200 just on such a happening. After all, it rose about $50 an ounce in the month or so after the announcement that the auction would be cut in half!

As to the second question, concerning the possible replenish- ment of the gold stockpile, this could only occur if the Adminis- tration wanted to restore gold partly to its rightful monetary role, as a reserve for something that reflects value. In Chauncey Depew's time (1904) there was $1 in gold for every $24 of paper money issued by the United States in circulation. Some econometrician figured out that by 1980 there would be $1 in gold in the Treasury for every $17,000 of paper floating around some- where in the world. Of course, we could not expect the Govern- ment suddenly to change bad habits bred from years and years of printing press activity. But if some form of fiscal sanity ever returns to Washington, perhaps the managers will realize that the less than 300 million ounces of gold in the Treasury ought to be beefed up with some buying, not selling. If such a miracle ensued it would add another $100 or $200 an ounce to the price of gold.

I claim no special knowledge on the third question: although my paternal grandfather was a flour miller in Minsk, he managed to emigrate to the United States in 1906 and my father, I and my sons of course are Americans; we have no pipeline to beyond the Iron Curtain. But from what I have read and observed it appears that the Russians have been selling plenty of gold on the free world market as the dollar price has worked higher these past few years. And whenever weather and labor conditions inside the Soviet Union are adverse they will need Western goods, including grains and certain metals like lead which are in short supply. Should this condition exist or compound, the extra Russian gold on the market may constrain prices despite continued inflation from oil-price pressure. Thus increased Soviet gold sales could be a future price deterrent. (Since January 1978 the United States International Trade Commission has kept a record of Soviet sales of gold and the facts can be obtained from that agency in Washington, although the reports may be a few months behind.)

In connection with the fourth question, concerning the ability of Washington to cope with inflation, it is quite obvious that at the time of writing the Administration would rather live with inflation than recession, because the problem of inflation has been attacked tokenwise since October 1978 by monetary methods (half-hearted interest rate increases by the Federal Reserve Board). But this attacked the symptom instead of the disease. The current inflation in America is a cost-push one, where labor wants higher wages and capital demands higher prices to achieve a return on money. There is only one way to stop inflation and that is, as Phil Lindstrom of Hecla Mining Company claims, to 'simply stop it'. This was done in time of war with mandatory wage/price controls that had teeth in them. It is almost certain that in the immediate future the Administration intends to stick to its voluntary wage/price controls, which, of course, haven't worked. Thus inflation will continue to rise in America and the price of gold should continue to appreciate as long as this rate is rising. Should a strong Administration take over the reins of government and ask Congress for powers to impose mandatory wage/price controls, then the prices of precious metals, including gold, will decline.

As to the fifth and final question posed earlier in this chapter, it is virtually certain that as long as the OPEC nations are loaded with dollars that keep depreciating in purchasing power, oil, which is traded around the world in dollars, will rise in price to compensate those countries not only for the loss of purchasing power on the dollars already in hand, but also on those received for the sale of the oil itself. Since the United States imports only about half its energy needs and this amount is less than 2% of the nation's gross national product, the rises in oil prices will affect Switzerland, West Germany and Japan even more deeply from an inflation point of view. In 1978, for example, the rate for Switzerland was 1½%, for West Germany, 2½%, and for Japan, 4%. At last look the German inflation rate had soared to 4% and Japan was headed for 6% because of the oil rise. It seems likely that OPEC will continue to meet regularly and to regularly increase the price of the oil they market.

So where will the price of gold go in the near future? Bernard Baruch used to say 'There's one thing sure about stocks. They'll continue to fluctuate in price'. The price of gold today is firmly locked to inflation and the cost of a barrel of oil. Right now it looks as if the rate of inflation worldwide and the price of oil worldwide have only one place to go, and that is *up*. So long as current conditions exist, the price of gold will keep rising. Naturally there will be setbacks along the way in day-to-day trading, caused by economic reports, by actions of governments and by large-scale buying and selling. So the basic trend in the price of the metal is bullish, but along the way gold will have its daily ups and downs and traders will make and lose money daily in both the physicals and the futures markets. As to supply/demand imbalances, Henry Jarecki has noted that 'the world's supplies of gold are enormous: 2½ billion ounces. This would suffice to supply the world's needs for fifty years if every mine in the world closed down tomorrow.'

As the price works higher new mines and new explorations designed to find new lodes will arise, yet no matter how much gold is dumped on to the marketplaces of the world it manages to disappear into the hands of some holder willing to resell it one day to somebody else for value. Still, the central issue for gold, as succintly stated by Dr. Jarecki, is that: 'Its destiny is its monetary character and its use as a store of value, not only for holders of dollars but also for holders of other currencies, many of which are far more vulnerable to the force of gravity than our currency.'

And on a note of caution that the force of gravity could also apply to the gold price if governments decide to make another Bre⁺:on Woods agreement, I end this book, wishing you the best of luck in making money on future gold fluctuations.

Epilogue

Since the text of this book was completed, the prices of gold and other precious metals have undergone extreme upside volatility. This has caused commodity exchanges and commission merchants to raise original and maintenance margins, reducing the leverage advantages of futures trading. Margins for spreads also have been altered accordingly.

That is why it is important for the reader to determine in advance precisely what amounts are necessary to accomplish strategies at the involved houses and also to maintain a sufficient cash reserve to weather adverse market conditions.

In addition, since this book was written, the United States has suspended its gold auctions, adding more uncertainties to the process. The political unrest in the Middle East and the constant pressure upwards on oil prices by OPEC nations preclude any significant setback to gold prices in the foreseeable future.

Moreover, there is a growing movement around the world to restore gold to its role as a reserve asset backing up paper money. How much effect this will have in the future on the price of gold is anybody's guess. But one thing is obvious. After my return from a European trip in late October, 1979, where I had a chance to talk with money people in London, Amsterdam, Hamburg, Geneva, Lugano and Zurich, I realized that no country is prepared to replace the dollar as the reserve currency upon which world trade revolves; and as I have pointed out in the text, there is no chance at all that gold will be remonetized as part of the United States currency. Thus, despite clamors from certain areas of the world for paper backed by gold, it is patently clear that the dollar will not return to the status it had before Franklin Delano Roosevelt's presidency.

On the other hand, if Americans become infected with the same kind of emotional attitude that has pervaded the European outlook for almost a thousand years, in regarding gold as the best kind of chaos hedge, then we shall see a constant buying base under the price for some years to come. Some traders from the short side will still make money, as well as lose it, and the timing of those trading from the long side will dictate their profits or losses.

In the meantime, if the trading 'lessons' in this book turn out to be of assistance, then the work will have been genuinely worthwhile.

Glossary

Arbitrage: A riskless transaction, usually performed by buillion-dealer exchange members, who may simultaneously buy in one gold market and sell in another, generating a profit through price differences.

Aside: Futures traders often find markets are such that they can go short-term either way; experience indicates that at such times the gold bull or bear might do better to simply be out of the market, or 'aside'.

Auctions: At one time there were two monthly gold auctions: (1) the IMF auction, involving 440,000 troy oz (2) the US Treasury auction (GSA) involving, when suspended in November, 1979, 750,000 oz of 900 gold. On the one hand the IMF auction was designed to help underdeveloped countries acquire gold to 'strengthen' their currencies; and on the other, the Treasury auctions were designed to aid in financial cosmetics by making the US balance of payments deficit figures look better.

Authenticity: The actual gold content in any lot in hand, authenticated by a reliable seller.

Backwardation market: A futures market where the far-out months trade at a discount on (less than) the nearby months because of tight supply in nearby metal. In this case demand exceeds near-term supply, a situation that has not yet arisen in the gold futures markets. See *Contango Market.*

Bar charts: Charts of gold futures prices reflecting time, price, volume, open interest, etc. Buy and sell signals are derived from trendlines and patterns made by daily highs and lows, or weekly or monthly prices, and by the patterns these prices form over a period of time.

Basis: See *Gold spreads*.

Bear spread: Sell front month, buy back month. Usually put on when a market is expected to change from a *Backwardation* market to a *Contango market*. See also *Gold spreads*.

Bull spread: Sell back month, buy front month. Usually put on when a normal *Contango market* is expected to change to a *Backwardation market*. See also *Gold spreads*.

Bullion: For the purpose of this book, bullion is 995–999 gold in any form from 1 kilogram bars to the standard 400 oz bar. Naturally, gold in purity less than 995 is also called bullion, but probably has to be refined to at least 995 level for ready resale.

Bullion coins: Coins struck from gold containing much less than 995 or 999 purity but containing sufficient 'fine gold' to act as a substitute for the bullion. These coins are designed to fill needs of gold buyers who may not have the means or the inclination to collect gold bars and ingots. The most popular bullion coins are the South African Krugerrand, the Austrian 100 Kroner, the British Sovereign, the Mexican 50 Peso and the French Napoleon. While the coins are generally restruck in order to meet demand, the Krugerrand is legal tender and the French Napoleon has not been restruck as yet. The future picture will be different because many countries, including Canada, the USSR and Third-World nations, have gone into the business of getting a premium for gold by striking bullion coins with a collector 'atmosphere'. Bullion coins carry as high as 10% premium over the cost of gold bullion.

Butterflies: A form of spreading that involves the simultaneous purchase of a near month and a far month with concurrent sale of two in-between months.

Buyer: A risk-taker who goes long in a future, or buys an option. An option buyer is also called a taker, holder or owner.

Buying hedge: See *Hedging*.

Carrying charge market: See *Contango market*.

Cash-and-carry: At one time the futures in gold a year or more out traded at a sufficiently higher price than the spot gold to permit investors to purchase gold bullion and simultaneously sell the gold futures a year or more out, 'locking in' the differential and earning a return on the money invested in the gold bullion without risk. This process was called cash-and-carry. When the cost of money was relatively cheap this strategy lended itself to financing of the bullion involved. But for the past few years the cost of money has been much higher than any advantage from this strategy and it has gone into limbo.

Charges: Whenever a merchant performs a service for a client there are generally charges. For example, there is no charge when a risk-taker goes long in a contract of September gold in July. But, come September, the customer wants to take actual possession of the gold represented by the contract. He will pay commissions, and delivery and transportation charges – and, if storage is desired, storage and insurance charges. It is always best to determine any charges in advance of incurring them.

Chaos hedge: See *Gold investor*.

Closing out: Liquidating and offsetting an existing long or short futures position, also known as 'exiting'.

Commission: In America there are no longer any fixed charges for a 'round-turn' futures transaction. Exchanges there do not levy any uniform charges and it is best to check with the futures commission merchant handling the proposed gold trade and determine what the charges for making the trade involve. Contrary to practice at stock brokerage firms, only one commission is charged to the risk-taker for each trade, upon liquidation of that position. Current charges for positioning and liquidating a single gold futures contract may vary from $50 to $75, depending on the firm and/or size of the account. See also *Round-turn*.

Contango market: A futures market in gold where the farther out months trade at higher prices than the nearby months, reflecting the normal carrying charges of the physical for the time involved. Carrying charges consist of theoretical interest, storage and insurance charges. The contango market is also called a 'normal' or 'carrying charge' market. Supply is equal to or exceeds near-term demand.

Contrarian: Only the game fish swims upstream, and contrarians are traders who trade against the herd of investors or speculators who go with the crowd.

Cover: When a trader or speculator is short in a gold future he offsets his obligation by buying a lot similar to the one sold short. This action is called 'short covering', or 'buying to cover'.

Day trade: Performing a round-turn within a trading session is called a day trade and usually commissions are half what they are for trades that exist longer on the books than a single session. Certain firms, however, charge the same rate for day trades as for overnight trades. The advantage of a day trade is that no margin is ever required, and the speculator takes any profit or supplies any loss involved.

Discount: The amount of money below the price of London gold a buyer may pay if purchasing gold during an auction or distress sale. See *Gold spreads*.

Dollar averaging: A method superior to arithmetical averaging in that whether the price of gold goes up or down a person using the same amount of dollars over a period of time who invested equal amounts of dollars would wind up with more gold than if he had mathematically averaged his purchases.

Econometric research: See *Statistical research*.

Elliott Wave System: A technical trading system invented by a chartist who believed that all prices act like waves in the ocean, rising and falling rhythmically. The magic number involved is five. After the fifth wave in a rising market there should be quite a collapse.

Equity: The value of a risk taker's commodity futures account.

Excess: The amount of money a customer maintaining a futures account can withdraw without liquidating the positions.

Exit: Synonymous with *Closing out*.

Fix: See *Gold fixing*.

Forward metal: Gold that has been contracted for delivery at some forward or precise future date. Normally such contracts are settled by delivery and payment precisely on the settlement (prompt) date.

Fundamental research: This is a study of the supply/demand, production/consumption of a specific commodity in order to attempt to assess where the price of the commodity will go. Generally, the fundamental researcher disregards market activity but concentrates on the 'numbers' in order to form conclusions as to price direction.

Futures: Contracts for the purchase or sale of a specific lot of a certain commodity at an agreed price for delivery any time during an assigned delivery month. These contracts are made between a buyer and a seller through members of a futures exchange and cleared through the clearing house utilized by the exchange. Performance is guaranteed by the clearing house and margins are received by the clearing house from both the seller and the buyer of any futures contract traded on the futures exchange to assure performance by the contracting parties.

Futures exchange: Membership organization whose activity involves trading sessions between members in the specific commodities listed for trading on the exchange. Operations of the exchanges are divided broadly into floor operations (trading) and clearing (processing the trades between members through the clearing house). In addition, of course, there are committees on membership, compliance, public relations, etc. For a thorough listing of futures exchanges round the world see: J. Edwards, ed. *Guide to World Commodity Markets*, Kogan Page, London, 1979.

Gold certificate: A certificate attesting to a person's ownership of a specific amount of bullion paid for and stored at some reliable depository. In the United States banks in New York and Chicago have created gold accumulation plans involving gold certificates in which participants can deposit dollars that are converted into gold stored at depositories selected by the banks. See Appendix B, p. 122.

Gold dealer: A synonym for a member of the London gold market, or any reputable affiliate of such a member, or agent of such a member. For the purposes of this book we do not include the people listed in the telephone company yellow pages under 'gold dealer.'

Gold fixing (gold fix): This is an event that occurs twice each trading day at the offices in London of N. M. Rothschild & Sons in a room occupied by five representatives of the five members of the London gold market. At about 10 a.m. London time (5 a.m. New York time) the first fixing occurs if a satisfactory price is agreed upon by the members. This price is then posted as the first fixing, popularly called the 'gold fix'. This morning fixing is followed at about 3 p.m. London time (10 a.m. New York time) with an afternoon fix. These fixes provide a reference price round the world as gold dealings take place. The wire services now monitor activity in the market in between fixes and after the fixes as dealing occurs in London between brokers and dealers. While London may not be the largest volume centre of gold trading these days it is still one of the most important because of the daily fixings that can and do influence prices on futures exchanges and in the physicals markets.

Gold funds: These are funds that pool investors' monies either in gold mining stocks or in bullion. A list may be had at any reliable brokerage firm.

Gold investments: These can be bullion, coins, collector coins, jewelry, gold *objets d' art,* or any other items like medallions which will be held to be passed on to heirs or liquidated in an estate. It is a rare case that a gold investment brings a profit to the investor while he or she is alive; gold investments are things that normally are never sold but held as hedges against inflation in paper money.

Gold investor: A person who is convinced that part of his or her assets should be placed in some form of physical bullion, or gold coins. It is normally the intent of an investor to leave the funds involved locked up in the gold medium in order to provide a 'chaos hedge', as Franz Pick terms it. According to him paper money will eventually either be reverse split or repudiated and the only refuge mankind can safely have when it comes to a storehouse of value is gold. Lately, Dr Pick has mellowed and admitted that silver and platinum group metals might also make satisfactory chaos hedges.

Gold options: For value received the grantor of the gold option is obliged to sell to the option buyer (holder, taker) a specific amount of gold at the agreed contract price (strike price) at any time during the life of the contract at the request of the buyer in the case of a *call*, or to receive delivery from the holder in the case of a *put*. The buyer of a bona fide gold put or call pays a money premium to the grantor for the privilege of either exercising his option or abandoning it if the market turns unfavorable. The only bona fide options at the time of writing are (1) Mocatta (2) Valeurs White Weld (3) Winnipeg. See Appendixes C and D, pp. 123–124.

Gold price: This is usually taken to be the price at one or the other of the two daily London fixings. When anyone asks 'What's the price of gold?' anywhere around the world, the London price is generally provided as the answer. See *Gold fixing*.

Gold shares: These include shares of stock in gold mining companies in South Africa and other countries around the world. Most of the free world gold comes from South Africa and the shares of their mining companies are sometimes classified under the rather insulting term 'Kaffirs'. Ethnic awareness will in time obliterate this nomenclature, but in the meantime these mines are classified according to their anticipated length of life (long, short and medium). Incidentally, the shorter the anticipated life of such a mine, generally, the more generous the dividend payout. But the danger of monetary loss when the dividends stop is all too evident.

Gold/silver ratio: The number of ounces of silver required at current spot prices to buy one ounce of spot gold.

Gold speculator: Unlike the gold investor, the gold speculator is intensely interested in making money from price fluctuations in gold bullion, futures, coins, etc. Since these media are paid for with paper money, the speculator hopes to be able to trade in and out of his positions profiting on balance and accumulating more paper, whether the paper be dollars, Sterling or francs.

Gold spreads: In normal ('carrying charge' or 'contango') markets gold futures reflect higher prices the further out the delivery month goes. Spreaders can possibly profit at times when the basis (*premium* or *discount*) between the months becomes distorted because of either excess activity or lack of activity in one or the other trading months. If the risk-taker believes the far-out month will rise slower and fall faster than the nearby month he puts on a *bear spread* (sells the nearby month and buys the far-out month). If he feels the far-out month will rise faster than the nearby month and decline slower than the nearby month he puts on a *bull spread* (sells the far-out month and buys the nearby month). In putting on the spreads the trader usually refers to the month trading at a premium to the other delivery month involved.

Gold trader: A professional person who spends all of his or her time trading in gold, either for their own account or for the account of a gold dealing firm. The term has also been broadened to include gold traders in the futures pits in New York and Chicago and on the floor of any other city in the world where gold is traded in an open outcry market.

Grantor/granter: See *Seller.*

Hedging: Protecting an existing position by making an opposite transaction. Also, in a commercial sense, protecting the needs of a firm from price fluctuations. Thus a firm that is a user of gold would probably make a *buying hedge* by contracting to purchase needed quantities of forward metal or futures; and a firm that produces metal might make a *selling hedge* by selling forward or going short in the futures in the amount required. In all cases – except where options are used for hedging purposes – the hedger is locked in for the duration of the hedge. That is, he cannot make or lose money on price fluctuations of the metal but is content with the protection offered by the hedging strategy.

Holder: See *Buyer.*

Inverted market: A synonym for *Backwardation market.*

Kaffirs: See *Gold shares.*

Leverage: Using other people's money, or buying and selling a lot of gold with a small deposit via futures or options. The UK term for leverage is *gearing.*

Leverage contracts: Thinly disguised substitutes for the banned commodity options in the United States. The contract usually provides for a forward delivery on a specific date of a set amount of gold at the pleasure of the buyer (taker). A substantial deposit is required at time of firming of the contract and the buyer is not obliged to accept the gold on the due date or lose any more than the deposits advanced if the price of gold drops. If, however, it rises and the buyer demands delivery or wants to resell the contracts back to the issuing firm for value, there is the risk that the firm might default. CFTC has ruled that in 1980 leverage contracts should be considered in the same light as futures. But we suggest readers avoid being involved at all with any kind of leverage or limited-risk forward contract.

Limited-risk forward contracts: Another gold options substitute: See *Leverage contracts.*

Locked in: When a futures trader is hedged and cannot get out without offsetting both sides of the hedge (spread). See *Hedging.*

London gold market: This select body of gold dealers consists of (1) Mocatta & Goldsmid (2) N. Rothschild & Sons (3) Johnson Matthey (4) Sharps Pixley (5) Samuel Montagu & Co.

Long: When a risk-taker buys a futures contract or gold bullion or a gold option he is considered to be 'long'. When he sells the futures or the physical he is said to have liquidated the long position. See also *Short.*

Longside trading: If the basic trend of gold is upwards, then traders will go long on weakness and sell on strength. This is trading the market from the long side. The reverse strategy is trading the market from the short side, or *Shortside trading.*

Maintenance margin: This is the money required by the broker to be supplied to the clearing house after a risk-taker's position becomes adverse. See also *Margin.*

Major trend: see *Price trend.*

Maker: See *Seller.*

Margin: The money deposit demanded by the rules of the various gold exchanges when a risk-taker goes long or short in a gold future. This deposit is termed 'original margin'; and, if the price in the market place does not favor the speculator's position, additional 'maintenance margin' is required. When gold spreads change their basis the risk-taker is required to deposit 'variation margin' in addition to the original margin deposited when the spreads were positioned.

Market correction: When gold has been overbought or oversold a market correction (price reversal) could be imminent.

Minor trend: See *Price trend.*

Momentum devices: Technical tools used in trading systems that forecast if a price movement in a specific direction will continue or will reverse.

Moving averages: Price composites charted on the same chart as daily or weekly prices and which are used by technical traders to support their theories of price advance/declines.

Normal market: See *Contango market.*

Offset: Whenever a trader is long or short in a gold future, the way the trade is exited is to make an opposite transaction in the future of the same delivery month and instruct the broker to 'offset'. This action will cancel the open position held at the clearing house. See also *Open interest, Closing out.*

Open interest: Suppose a gold trader at Conti goes long in one December Comex gold futures contract, in August; the seller of the contract is Bache's customer. The Comex clearing house now registers Conti as being long in one December gold at the trade price and Bache as being short at the same price. The open interest at the exchange has been added to by *one*. Thus by definition a single open interest at the clearing house represents one long and one short that are *open*. Now if gold goes up or down in the next few days after the trade and Conti's customer decides to liquidate the long by selling, but Bache's customer decides to remain short, the open interest will not change because a new long, from, say, Thomson McKinnon, will replace Conti's long. Of course, if Conti and Bache both got rid of their customer's open positions then the open interest at the clearing house would be reduced by one. Open interest is an important technical tool for traders interested in market dynamics. If the open interest is increasing and the price is increasing there is still room on the upside for the gold price. If the open interest is increasing and the price is falling there is still room on the downside for the price of gold. If the price increases but the open interest decreases or remains flat the chances are that a price reversal will occur soon. If the price decreases and the open interest decreases or remains flat, a reversal or rebound is likely.

Open outcry: Each order to buy or to sell in an organized futures exchange regulated by the CFTC must be orally declared at time of the trade including the appropriate exchange hand signals.

Original margin: See *Margin*.

Overbought: When gold has run up enthusiastically and the open interest suddenly begins to falter and decline the commodity is said to have been overbought and a reaction is imminent.

Overnight trade: Any position, long or short, that remains on a broker's books more than a day is called an overnight trade and is usually charged at double the day-trade rate. Overnight trades, of course, require initial or outright margin and subsequent maintenance margin may be needed. See also *Day trade*.

Oversold: When gold has dropped alarmingly and the open interest suddenly starts to decrease the commodity is said to have been oversold and a rally is imminent.

Point-and-figure charts: A charting system that examines only price and disregards time and volume. This system is designed to indicate imminent reversals and permit the trader to forecast when to go long or short by estimating price objectives through box counts and interpretations of chart patterns.

Points: Futures trade by advancing and declining each trading day in dollars or parts of dollars per ounce. These parts are called points. A hundred point advance in a gold future is equivalent to $1 rise in the price per ounce on the exchange. Thus, a trader who has to pay $50 for a round-turn commission on a 100 ounce gold contract needs at least a favorable 50-point move in any long or short position to break even. Obviously, if the trader can arrange for a $20 round-turn he can go in and out the market quite frequently and scalp small profits or escape with small losses. See also *Commission*.

Premium: The amount of money above the price of spot gold a buyer may have to pay if purchasing gold in bullion coin form, or in less than London gold market trading quantities (2000–4000 ounces at an order). See also *Gold spreads*.

Price trend: A technical trading term presuming the future direction of the price of a commodity future, including gold. This trend is projected by various methods, including 'trendlines' connecting tops and bottoms on price charts and moving averages. It is again divided into the major trend (long-term projected price trend) and the minor trend (short-term projected price objectives).

Resistance: In technical trading, a price area where new selling will emerge to dampen a continued rise. See also *Support, Technical trading.*

Reversals: Price points where the direction reverses. In the formation of point and figure charts, the chart-maker decides how many points to make his reversals. For example, a gold chartist may decide $3 per ounce change as a reversal for his point and figure chart and will begin plotting in that manner. Assuming gold goes up $2 on the first day, $4 the next day and $2 the third day, then the chartist, will insert **X**s along the same vertical axis. On the fourth day gold falls back $2 and the chartist does nothing. On the fifth day it drops another $3 and then he places an **O** on the vertical line next to the **X**s at the price at which gold traded. The **O** was placed to signify a down day that was in line with the $3 reversal scheme set up for the chart. See also *Technical trading.*

Round-turn (round-trip): The installation of a long or short futures position and the subsequent exiting of such position is called a round-turn or round-trip.

Seller: A risk-taker who sells a future position short, or grants (sells) a commodity option. An option seller is also called a maker, grantor or granter.

Selling hedge: See *Hedging.*

Settlement date: See *Forward metal.*

Settlement price: This is the price at which the futures trading in gold for each listed month is officially closed at the end of each trading session.

Short: When a risk-taker thinks the price of a gold future is too high he can effect a sale of the future, hoping to enter the market when it gets lower and buy a similar lot to cover. If, however, the market rises he is required to supply maintenance margin, but can cancel his obligation by buying a lot similar to the futures sold and pairing off the trade. See also *Long, Maintenance margin, Offset.*

Short covering: See *Cover.*

Shortside trading: If the basic trend of gold is down, then traders will sell short on rallies and cover on subsequent weakness. This is trading the market from the short side, or shortside trading. The reverse strategy is *Longside trading.*

Spot gold: The going price of gold in the cash market. Normally, the price of the fixing in London is assumed round the world to be the spot price but there may be slight variations depending on the location of the *Spot market* being quoted.

Spot market: The actual market for cash purchase of bullion on any specific day anywhere in the world. The spot price will vary from market to market: thus, Zurich may abide by the London fix, but New York may adhere to Handy & Harman's, Engelhard's or Mocatta's quotation. See also *Gold fixing, Gold price.*

Statistical research: Proliferation of computer usage has spawned econometric research, or application of statistical, mathematical equations to commodity research. The use of multiple regressions and computer programs to make price predictions typifies this kind of research.

Strong currencies: Currencies that reflect economies of countries in better shape than that of the United States. Such currencies include the Swiss Franc, the German Mark and the Japanese Yen, at present.

Supply/demand equation: With respect to the price of a physical commodity, this equation states that if supply exceeds demand then the price should decline and if demand exceeds supply the price should rise. If supply and demand are equal the price should be stable.

Support: In technical trading, a price area where new buying will probably come in and stem any decline. See also *Resistance, Technical trading.*

Switch: When a long or short in gold futures nears the spot month something is normally done to avoid delivery and remain in the market. The liquidation of the near-month future position and replacement by a farther-out month is therefore called a switch.

Taker: See *Buyer*.

Technical research: A study of market dynamics utilizing one or more technical trading systems. See *Technical trading*.

Technical trading: Systematic trading based on charts that reveal buy and sell signals. The 'technician' firmly believes that the fundamentals are expressed in the market price and that money can be made by interpreting market action and forecasting that action based on the charting system utilized.

Trendlines: See *Price trend*.

Triple 9: The highest purity of gold bullion, 99.9% pure gold. Soviet gold is marketed in this form, whereas South African gold usually appears in 99.5% form.

Variation margin: This was the name for interim margin on a daily basis that had to be supplied when cash-and-carries were involved. It has also been applied to the kind of margin required to maintain existing gold spreads when the basis of the spreads changes. See also *Cash-and-carry, Margin*.

Weak currencies: The opposite of *Strong currencies;* currencies of countries with weaker economies than that of the United States.

Appendixes

Appendix A: Official list of New York Comex approved brands and markings

Producer	Refined at	Brand marks
All Union Gold Factory	(Soviet Union)	CCCP (with hammer and sickle)
Argor, SA	Chiasso, Switzerland	ARGOR SA CHIASSO (with SAA)
ASARCO Incorporated	Amarillo, Texas	ASARCO GOLD-AMARILLO TEXAS
	Perth Amboy, NJ	ASARCO-PERTH AMBOY
Canadian Copper Refiners Ltd	Montreal East, Quebec, Canada	CANADIAN COPPER REFINERS LTD
Compagnie des Métaux Précieux	Paris, France	COMPAGNIE DES METAUX PRECIEUX-PARIS

(Bars produced for Société de Banque Suisse will also contain assayer's stamp 'SBS')

Comptoir Lyon-Alemand Louyot	Noisy Le Sec, France	COMPTOIR-LYON-ALEMAND, LOUYOT-PARIS
Deutsche Gold und Silber Schneideanstalt Vormals Roessler	Frankfurt, West Germany	DEGUSSA
H. Drijfhout & Zoon's Edelmetaalbedrijven N.V.	Amsterdam-Centre, Netherlands	

Engelhard Industries Ltd	Cinderford, Gloucestershire, UK	ENGELHARD LONDON (with large letter 'E')
Engelhard Industries Pty Ltd	Thomastown, Victoria, Australia	ENGELHARD INDUSTRIES PTY. LTD. AUSTRALIA (also 'ASSAY OFFICE' with large letter 'E' within octagon)
Engelhard Industries of Canada Ltd	Aurora, Ontario, Canada (formerly produced at Toronto, Ontario)	ENGELHARD (with circle connected to half-moon)
Engelhard Mining & Chemical Corp.	Newark, NJ	ENGELHARD (with large letter 'E')
	Newark, NJ	BAKER
Handy & Harman	Attleboro, Mass.	HH HANDY & HARMAN
W. C. Heraeus GmbH	Hanau am Main, West Germany	
Homestake Mining Company	Lead, South Dakota	HMC HOMESTAKE MINING COMPANY (within circle)
Johnson Matthey Limited (formerly Johnson Matthey & Mallory Ltd)	Brampton, Ontario, Canada	JM CANADA (with crossed hammers)
	Brampton, Ontario, Canada	JOHNSON MATTHEY & MALLORY-CANADA (no longer produced)
Johnson Matthey Chemicals Ltd	Royston, Hertfordshire, UK	JOHNSON MATTHEY LONDON
Johnson Matthey & Pauwels SA	Brussels, Belgium	JOHNSON MATTHEY AND PAUWELS
Matthey Bishop, Inc.	Winslow, NJ	MATTHEY BISHOP U.S.A.

(Also distributes Johnson Matthey London brand in US)

Matthey Garrett Pty Ltd	Kogarah, New South Wales, Australia	MATTHEY GARRETT PTY-SYDNEY

Métaux Précieux SA	Neuchatel, Switzerland	METAUX PRECIEUX SA (with refiner's assay stamp 'MP')
(Bars produced for Société de Banque Suisse will contain assayer's stamp 'SBS')		
Metalli Preziosi SpA	Paderno Dugnano (Milan), Italy	METALLI PREZIOSI SpA (with MP inside a diamond)
NV Metallurgie Hoboken-Overpelt SA	Hoboken, Antwerp, Belgium	METALLURGIE HOBOKEN OVERPELT
	Hoboken, Antwerp, Belgium	SOCIETE GENERALE METALLURGIQUE DE HOBOKEN (no longer produced)
	Hoboken, Antwerp, Belgium	METALLURGIE HOBOKEN (no longer produced)
Norddeutsche Affinerie	Hamburg, West Germany	NORDDEUTSCHE AFFINERIE HAMBURG
The Perth Mint	Perth, Western Australia	THE PERTH MINT AUSTRALIA (with swan motif mint mark within circle)
Rand Refinery Ltd	Germiston, Transvaal	THE RAND REFINERY LTD (circled around a picture of a spring-bok)
Royal Canadian Mint	Ottawa, Ontario	ROYAL CANADIAN MINT (encircling a crown)
Schone Edelmetaal BV		
Sheffield Smelting Co. Ltd	Sheffield, UK	THE SHEFFIELD SMELTING CO. LTD. – LONDON & SHEFFIELD
State Refinery	Moscow, USSR	CCCP (with hammer and sickle)

United States Assay Office	New York City, NY San Francisco, Cal. (no longer producing)	Seal of United States within circle with year and location of production
United States Metals Refining Co.	Carteret, NJ	DRW
United States Mint	Philadelphia, Pa. Denver, Colorado	Seal of United States within circle with year and location of production (no longer produced)
Valcambi SA	Balerna, Switzerland	VALCAMBI (with refiner's assay stamp 'CHI')
	Balerna, Switzerland	CREDIT SUISSE (with refiner's assay stamp 'CHI')

Appendix B: Mocatta Delivery Orders (DOs)

Issued on:
20 South African Krugerrands
1 kilo gold bar (32.15 troy ounces)
1 100 troy ounce gold bar
1 400 troy ounce gold bar
Negotiable in larger unit quantities (10 or more) on the following units:
20 Mexican 50 Peso gold pieces
1 1000 troy ounce silver bar
1 $1000 face value silver clad coin bag

Issued by: Mocatta Metals Corporation

Depositories: MAT Securitas Express Ltd, Zurich, Switzerland; Wilmington Trust Company, Wilmington, Delaware.

Storage charges: ½% per year for first to fifth year, 2% per year thereafter (minimum one year). Storage is paid via purchase of storage stamps to be affixed to reverse of Delivery Order.

Delivery Order issuance charge: $100 per Delivery Order plus ½% (storage) prorated for unused part of current year.

Out charges: $20 per unit.

Total purchase price: Mocatta sales price for metal or coins plus $100 Delivery Order issuance charge plus prorated storage charge plus broker's commission. For example, if Mocatta offers 100 ounce gold bar at $500 per ounce, a Delivery Order bought on July 1 will cost buyer:

Mocatta sales price for metal	$50,000
Delivery Order issuance charge	100
Prorated storage charge (½ % for half year)	250
Total to Mocatta	$50,350
Broker's commission (say, 3 % of $50,000)	1,500
Total paid by customer	$51,850

A free booklet describing more fully the details of these Delivery Orders is available from any authorized agent of Mocatta.

Appendix C: Mocatta gold options

Available options: calls and puts.

Grantor: Mocatta Metals Corporation.

Quantity: 100 troy ounces, 995 gold.

Equivalence: one Comex, IMM or CBOT futures contract.

Strike price increments: $10 per ounce, at, above and below market.

Expirations: up to 16 months forward on the first trading day of March, June, September and December.

Mocatta also grants calls on lots of 50 Krugerrands, equivalent to 50 ounces of fine gold, in $10 strike differentials for the months of January, April, June and November.

For full details of Mocatta options and how they can be applied to trading situations see 'A short course in Mocatta options', available from any authorised Mocatta agent.

Appendix D: Winnipeg gold options

Options available: centum gold.

Quantity: 100 troy ounces.

Strike price intervals: $10 per ounce.

Expiration months: March, June, September and December.

Commissions: $35 per option.

Trading hours: 8.15 a.m. to 1.30 p.m., Central time.

Winnipeg options were the only listed gold options traded in the world at the time this book was being written. They made their début in late spring 1979, and it is too early to be able to make a study of their effectiveness or fairness of premiums. All options are granted through the clearing house on behalf of the Winnipeg Exchange.

Free literature and a disclosure statement may be obtained by writing directly to the Winnipeg Commodity Exchange, 678–167 Lombard Avenue, Winnipeg, Manitoba R3B OV7 (phone 204-942-6401), for the attention of P. K. Huffman, Secretary-Treasurer.

Index